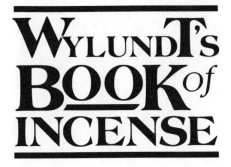

WYLUNDT'S
BOOK of
INCENSE

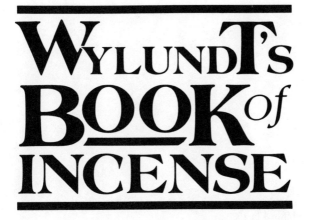

WYLUNDT'S BOOK of INCENSE

A MAGICAL PRIMER

Steven R. Smith

SAMUEL WEISER, INC.
York Beach, Maine

First published in 1989 by
Samuel Weiser, Inc.
Box 612
York Beach, Maine 03910

Library of Congress Cataloging-in-Publication Data

Smith, Steven R.
    Wylundt's book of incense.

    Bibliography: p.
        1. Incense--Miscellanea.   2. Magic--Miscellanea.
3. Astrology--Miscellanea.   I. Title.   II. Title:
Book of incense.
TP983.S66   1989   133.4'3   89-5827

ISBN 0-87728-679-5
Typeset in 10 pt. Caledonia
Printed in the United States of America by
Capital City Press

To Kun

CONTENTS

Appendices

ACKNOWLEDGMENTS

I'd like to take this opportunity to thank some of the many people who have helped to make this book possible. Without their help and support, this book would still be but a dream.

My thanks and gratitude go to Yoppy. Though no politician, she's had to spend time in smoke filled rooms. Qusil, a close friend whom I've never met. Ashi, who took in a stray and fed his spirit. Belus and Angelique, my brother and sister in all but blood.

Special thanks to Ellen Hansen, the *Pegasus Express*, and Karen Charboneau. Many of their recipes appear here through their courtesy. Recipes by Ellen Hansen are marked by asterisk(*), recipes by Karen Charboneau are marked by dagger(†).

INTRODUCTION

When I first began to make my own incense, I knew very little about it. Most of my experience has been gained through trial and error. This book will provide you with all types of incense recipes, so you won't have to make the same mistakes I've made.

This book is a primer, designed to help you build a solid base. Once you have mastered the techniques shown here, you can improve on them. Feel free to rearrange any of these recipes and methods to suit your personal tastes and needs.

You'll find complete instructions for making loose, cone, stick and cylinder incense, how to dry and store it, and how to gather, dry and store fresh herbs, plus a complete listing of herbs. I have included different kinds of incense recipes, providing recipes that are made for their fragrance and/or color, incense used for its astrological, magical or ritualistic correspondences. You can even learn to make liquid scents.

For the reader's convenience, I have included a list of the common names of herbs and plants, so you can cross-reference familiar names with the proper herbal listing. Also included is a list of planetary correspondences, a list of the magical uses of herbs. As you work with the recipes you may want to increase or decrease the proportions so in addition to an explanation of weights and measures, you will find appendices showing you how to adjust your recipes.

This book was not written with any particular doctrine in mind; it was written as a practical reference book for students of many diverse paths.

Part
One

MAKING
AND
USING
INCENSE

TYPES OF INCENSE

There are four basic forms of incense—loose, cone, cylinder, and stick. Each of these forms has its own advantages and disadvantages.

Loose incense is by far the oldest, most popular, and easiest form of incense to make and use. It is made by combining one or more herbs and/or spices, which are then burned directly over a heat source. The heat is usually supplied by self-lighting charcoal.

Although it is very easy to make and use, there are several disadvantages to using loose incense. The main disadvantage is waste. Herbs burn quickly and must be renewed frequently when burned directly over charcoal. Smoke is another problem. If loose incense is burned often, or for any length of time, your ceilings and furniture will get sooty and the room will smell like smoke.

As loose incense is usually burned on charcoal, this creates a potential fire hazard. Charcoal gives off a great deal of heat, which might ignite nearby flammable objects. Burning charcoal also gives off a toxic gas, which can cause severe headaches when burned in an enclosed area.

Despite these disadvantages, loose incense is by far the most versatile, the possible herb and/or spice combinations and variations available are virtually unlimited. Using loose incense and charcoal is also an easy way to experiment with blends and recipes. In the time it takes just one charcoal briquette to burn (approximately 1½ hours), you can experiment with dozens of herb, spice, and scent combinations.

Cone incense is another popular form of incense, and is the main form covered in this book. Many stores no longer carry cones, and those that do stock only a limited variety of scents.

Cone incense is self-burning and needs no charcoal. The possible blends and varieties of cones are almost limitless.

Cone incense is easier to use, more economical, and less messy than loose incense.

There are two main disadvantages to using cone incense. One is that it must be made by hand, which is time consuming. The other disadvantage is that the cone must be self-burning, and when you experiment with various ingredients, you may find that your incense won't burn!

Cylinder incense is similar to cone incense in that they both are made from basically the same ingredients and are usually formed by hand. Cylinders are longer and thinner than cones, and burn at a steadier rate and for a longer length of time.

The main disadvantages of cylinders are that they are hard to form, are sometimes very brittle, and all the ingredients must be in powdered form.

The longest burning form of incense is stick incense and it's the most economical to use. Another plus is that it can be partially burned, put out, then reused at another time.

Stick incense has its disadvantages, too. It is messy and hard to form. It usually is also hard to keep lit, unless you add some saltpeter when you make it. Stick incense must be dried slowly to prevent it from cracking. Much of its scent may be lost during the drying process.

INGREDIENTS NEEDED
TO MAKE INCENSE

With the exception of loose incense, all forms of incense need four basic ingredients: an aromatic substance, a base and/or chemical to help keep it burning, a bonding agent to hold it together, and a liquid to change the bonding agent into a glue.

Aromatic Substance

Any herb, spice, or scent that will give off a pleasing smell and/or cause a desired effect to occur when it is burned. Almost any kind of substance imaginable can and has been used as an aromatic substance. A listing of many of the more popular substances is included in part 2, as well as instructions for gathering, drying and storing herbs.

Base

Once you have chosen the fragrance you wish to use, you should then decide on a base. A base is a substance that burns easily and gives off either a pleasant aroma or no aroma at all when it is burned. The use of a base is necessary because most herbs burn poorly without one. The base also helps take the bitterness out of an herb, or makes its fragrance milder. Many herbs are too strong, pungent, bitter, or overpowering when burned by themselves. A good base will usually correct these faults, while still retaining the basic scent of the herb. The most popular and easy to obtain bases are wood powder, sandalwood, red sandalwood, quassia, vetiver, willow, evergreen needles, and talc.

Wood powder is nothing more than sawdust that has been ground very fine. You can either buy it or make your own. Any lumber store will be more than happy to give you all the sawdust you can use.

To make wood powder, put a cup of dry clean sawdust into a blender. Set the blender on chop and let it run for about two minutes. When done, sift the sawdust and save the fine powder in an airtight container. Never put sticks or wood chips in a blender, as it will damage the blades and/or burn out the motor.

The sawdust you get from a lumber store is usually pine. If you know people who cut their own firewood, you may be able to get some wild cherry or cedar sawdust, which will add a pleasing scent to most blends of incense. For that matter, sawdust from any type of fruit tree makes an excellent base material.

Being easily obtainable and quite inexpensive, wood powder is a popular base material. Its major drawback is that it leaves a strong and lingering burnt wood smell after it has been burned.

Sandalwood is by far the most popular and versatile of bases. Its sweet, clean, and woody aroma compliments almost any herb, spice, or fragrance. Unlike wood powder, sandalwood leaves no burny after-smell. Instead, it leaves a sweet and slightly floral aroma. Sandalwood may cost more than any other base, but it's well worth the price.

Red sandalwood is a different species of tree than sandalwood; but smells a lot like it. Its one minor drawback is its color, for it will add a reddish tint to any blend.

Quassia is also similar to sandalwood in scent, only not as strong or sweet. It is a very hard wood, so it must be purchased in powdered form, or it will be almost useless for incense making.

Vetiver smells much like sandalwood, only it is sweeter and not as clean smelling. Like quassia, it is hard and can only be used in powdered form.

Willow is an excellent base because it burns cleanly, with very little smoke and almost no scent. This makes it ideal for use in any blend. Its only bad point is that it burns very quickly, but this can be easily remedied by using less of it.

The needles from evergreen trees, especially pine, fir, and cedar, make a pleasant smelling base. They add a woodsy outdoors kind of scent to your incense. Evergreen needles can be easily powdered in a blender. Just put a cup of dried needles in a blender, set it on chop, and run it for about two minutes. When done, sift and store the powder in an airtight container. Never put twigs or needles that aren't completely dried in the blender. This can damage or gum-up the machine.

Because of their strong scent, evergreen needles aren't as versatile as most bases; their aroma will sometimes clash with other fragrances, particularly floral scents.

Most bases are used to help herbs to burn; but talc is an exception to the rule. It is used to lengthen burning time. Care should be taken not to add too much talc, or the blend may not burn at all.

There are many other substances that can be used as a base. Any material used for a base must burn easily and help sweeten or weaken (but not overpower) the fragrance of the aromatic substance being burned.

Potassium Nitrate

There are many herbs that are hard to burn, even with the aid of a base. For herbs like this, a burnable substance in addition to a base is needed. This substance is a chemical called potassium nitrate. It is also known by the names of niter and saltpeter.

It is not necessary to use saltpeter in loose incense. However, most cones and cylinders with two or more ingredients usually need some. Stick incense almost always needs it.

By adding saltpeter, the burning times of your incense is reduced by 25 percent to 40 percent, depending on the amount of saltpeter used and the ingredients of the blend. Saltpeter is not to be added directly to the dry ingredients. It should first be dissolved in the liquid that is to be used in the making of the cone, cylinder, or stick. This will give your incense a more even distribution of saltpeter, thus preventing smokey flare-ups. The proper methods of preparing saltpeter will be covered in the next chapter.

Bonding Agents

After you have chosen a fragrance and base, you will need something to "glue" them together so that you can form cones, cylinders, or sticks. For this you need a bonding agent. There are dozens of resins and gums which can be used for this purpose. To narrow down the field somewhat, the bonding agent should meet all of the following requirements:

1) It must be water soluble and quick dissolving.

2) It should be in a solid (powdered) form.

3) It should have little or no scent of its own when burned.

4) It should be easy to use and handle.

5) It shouldn't revert to its powdered form when dried.

6) It should be safe to use and non-toxic when burned.

There are nine gums that meet all six requirements. They are agar agar, ghatti gum, guar gum, gum arabic, locust bean gum, karaya, sodium alginate, tragacanth, and xanthan gum.

We can further eliminate five of these gums because they are only sold in bulk (100 lb. lots) to large food, drug, and cosmetic manufacturers: ghatti gum, guar gum, locust bean gum, sodium alginate, and xanthan gum.

Agar agar is readily available to the small consumer; however, it is very expensive. It costs nearly three times more than any other bonding agent.

Karaya is the least expensive gum listed. For this reason it is widely used by incense making companies. It usually comes in small chunks that must be ground to powder and dissolved in boiling water.

Gum arabic has been used for centuries for bonding incense. First, because it was the best available gum at the time; later it was used because it was called for in old recipes. It is still quite popular and is used by many amateur incense makers. Although gum arabic is a good bonding agent, it has two small faults: it is very sticky and messy to work with; and it rises to the surface of the incense as it dries. This leaves the center virtually gum-free and causes the incense to become brittle and break easily.

Tragacanth is by far the best available bonding agent. It dissolves easily and isn't sticky or messy to work with. All the recipes requiring a bonding agent that we will work with are designed to be made with tragacanth.

Tragacanth is a safe and versatile substance. It can be used to thicken gravy. Pharmaceutical companies use it to make pills, and cosmetic firms have used it in toothpaste, hand lotion, eye make-up, and shaving cream. Its only drawback is that it costs more than most other bonding agents. But, because of its superior bonding ability, only half as much is needed.

Liquid

You need a liquid to turn the bonding agent into a glue. The best and easiest liquid to use is water, but almost any fluid may be used. Such strange ingredients as wine, brandy, rose water, olive oil, and even beer can be used.

MAKING INCENSE

Incense is something that, when burned, gives off an agreeable odor and/or produces a desired effect. It can only do this if the proper aromatic substance is used. In this section we will go into more depth discussing these substances, because the proper choice and use of an aromatic substance is essential to the success of any blend.

The following is a brief description of the basic scents of different forms of aromatic substances. It is not all inclusive, and there are numerous exceptions.

Bark: woody, semisweet, mild
Berries: heavy, earthy, resin-like
Flowers: dry, grassy, semisweet
Gums: heavy, semisweet, resin-like
Leaves: dry, herby, grassy
Roots: earthy, heavy, woody, different
Seeds: burny, bitter, smokey
Spices: sweet, dry, mild
Wood: woody, semisweet, mild

Many herbs smell quite pleasant in their natural state, yet can be very offensive when burned. A good example of this is mint. Nothing smells as clean, fresh, and cool as mint leaves; however, when burned, mint smells awful.

The best way to tell how a prospective herb will smell in incense is to burn a little of it by itself. If the smell is agreeable, then you should use it. If it is not, then try its herbal scent, essence, or oil.

Before continuing, I would like to address those of you who suffer from hay fever, asthma, or have skin problems. The making and using of incense may cause some adverse effects. The problems it can cause aren't usually severe or long lasting; and because of the small amounts used, may not occur at all. While no two people react in the same way, it is fairly safe to say that in most cases the making or using of incense will have little or no effect on your general health, unless the substance used is either poisonous or narcotic — both of which should be avoided.

There is no such thing as the perfect incense formula — one that can be used successfully for every kind of herb, spice, flower, or blend. However, an excellent basic formula to begin your incense making with is one of twenty parts aromatic substance, four parts base, and one part bonding agent. This general formula can be used as a kind of stepping-stone to more elaborate formulas.

Always keep the proportion of aromatic substance at least twice as large as the base. The only exceptions to this rule are when you are working with an extremely strong or bitter herb, or if you are using only scents. (More will be said about scents in a later chapter.) The use of too much base, especially if it is wood powder, will leave a strong after-smell of smoke.

When you are just starting out or when making experimental blends, always make small batches. This will cut down on waste due to non-burning blends or blends that don't meet with your approval. Just a pinch or two of an ingredient is all you really need to find out if it smells good. Sprinkle a little on a lit charcoal briquette to find out how it will smell.

Many of the old traditional recipes give the impression that their ingredients and proportions must be carried out to the letter. There is nothing wrong with this, but I prefer to find out for myself. Whenever I come across a new recipe, I try it as it is recorded, then experiment with it by changing its proportions and by adding or subtracting ingredients. Feel free to experiment with any recipe in this book. After all, that's how most new recipes are either discovered or improved upon: by trial and error.

A beginner experimenting with blends should start by using equal amounts of each aromatic substance. Later, after you've gained more experience you can adjust the blends to suit your own tastes or needs. As your knowledge grows you can make your own blends by relying solely on your past experiments, experience, and insight.

Whenever you are measuring ingredients, always use level teaspoons, tablespoons, etc. In this way the measurements will always be accurate and you can easily reproduce any desired blend.

When making incense—be it cone, cylinder, or stick—the ingredients should always be ground as finely as possible. This will make the incense easier to work with and the finished product will burn cleaner and more evenly. For grinding down small amounts of ingredients, a mortar and pestle should be used. For larger quantities, a blender works nicely. After you have finely ground your ingredient, it should be sifted to remove any unground pieces. You can use anything from a hand-held flour sifter to a piece of screen. Even an old aluminum pie plate, with holes punched in it, will do the job.

Although many herbs will burn without a base, it is best to assume that one is needed, especially when working with blends. As stated earlier, a good starting formula is twenty parts aromatic substance, four parts base, and one part bonding agent.

As you already know, a base is sometimes used to keep an herb's scent from being too overpowering. Sometimes too much fragrance is just as bad as not enough. Whether or not you choose to use a base—or how much you use—is really a matter of personal taste. You are the artist, and the incense is your creation.

With the exception of saltpeter, all your dry ingredients should be mixed thoroughly before adding any liquid. I always use wooden popsicle sticks when mixing ingredients. Sticks may be purchased at almost any hobby or craft store. Whether mixing just dry ingredients, or later when liquid is added, these sticks are easy to use and keep clean. The incense ingredients will not adhere to them, as they would to a spoon or any other kind of mixing tool.

Liquid is added to incense to change the bonding agent from a dry powder into a glue. It is also used to dissolve saltpeter. The initials that you will see throughout this book are a code for water and saltpeter solutions. Please use the following measurements when adding a bonding agent to your recipe:

QB (Quarter Blend):   Make your liquid by combining the following:

water $1/2$ cup
saltpeter $1/4$t

FW (Fire Water):   water 8t
saltpeter $1/4$t

LF (Liquid Fire):   water 4t
saltpeter $1/4$t

For all types of bonding agents, after the saltpeter has been thoroughly dissolved, add the liquid to the dry ingredients. The proper amount of liquid to use is given in each recipe. Mix all the ingredients again with your "popsicle" stick, then knead it with your fingers.

The consistency of the incense mixture should be that of a soft lumpy putty or of moist dough. It should be easily workable, yet not too wet. If the mixture is too wet, the incense will run and sag. If it's too dry, it will be crumbly and hard to shape.

For a typical $2^{1/2}$ teaspoon dry mixture, a rough estimate of the amount of water to use is as follows:

For leaves and/or flowers use 1–$1^{1/4}$ teaspoons.

For roots use $1^{1/2}$–2 teaspoons.

For powdered herbs and spices use $1^{1/2}$–$1^{3/4}$ teaspoons.

Base and scent mixtures need $1^{1/2}$–2 teaspoons.

All others need from $1^{1/4}$–$1^{1/2}$ teaspoons of liquid.

If you aren't sure how much liquid to use, start with one teaspoon of fluid and then, if more is needed, add $1/4$ teaspoon at a time until the mixture is moist and workable

Cones

After you have thoroughly mixed and kneaded the incense mixture, break off a piece and form it into a cone shape. It should be about 1³/₄ inches long and ⁷/₁₆ inch in diameter at its base. It should resemble a tall, thin, inverted ice-cream cone (with one scoop of ice-cream on it). Hold it vertically and press the rounded end gently on a flat surface. Rounding before pressing will prevent the end from flaring out when flattened.

As the water in cone incense evaporates, the cone shrinks. The more water used, the more it will shrink. The average cone will lose about ¹/₈ inch in length and ¹/₁₆ inch in diameter.

Burning time depends almost entirely on the length of a cone, not on its thickness. Most cones will burn from 10 to 25 minutes, depending on the ingredients used and the size of the cone. Cones should be kept as thin as possible. This greatly reduces drying time and insures a more even burn.

When experimenting or making more than one blend at a time, it is wise to record the ingredients used and their proportions. Record also any comments or ideas that you may have, for future reference. Good record keeping will aid you greatly in your work. Even if an experiment is unsuccessful, record it and learn from your mistakes so you won't make the same error again.

Cylinders

After you have mastered the making of cone incense, you may wish to try your hand at making cylinders. Cylinder incense is very similar to cone incense in both manufacture and ingredients. Other than their obvious difference in shape, the only real difference between them is that all of the ingredients used in making cylinders *must* be in powder form. Powdered ingredients are necessary for the shaping and even burning of cylinders.

Being longer and thinner than cones, cylinders burn longer and at a more steady rate. Also, you can get more cylinders out of the same amount of ingredients. Use the same recipe as for cones. Use the amount of liquid that the recipe calls for, and then add a little plain water until the mixture is moist enough to easily work.

To form a cylinder, break off a piece of incense mixture and roll it gently on a clean smooth surface. Work it as you would a piece of clay. At first you will probably have some trouble forming cylinders, but it will become quite easy to do with practice. While any size cylinder will do, the most suitable size is one approximately 2³/₄ inches long and about ⁵/₁₆ inch in diameter. This size is small enough to work easily, yet large enough to burn for a long time.

If you want to add a professional look to your cylinders, they may be formed by using a cake decorator. If you have a plastic or tin one, all you need do is enlarge the hole in one of the removable spout attachments. The hole should be widened to no less than ⁵/₁₆ inch and no more than ³/₈ inch. Incense won't flow through if the hole is too small, and the cylinders will be too large if the hole is too wide.

Form the cylinders on a smooth hard surface. When they begin to set up (in about half an hour) roll them over 180 degrees. Roll them again in about another hour. This will prevent the cylinders from sticking to your drying board.

Cylinders, because they are much thinner than cones, will dry in about half the time. On a warm summer's day, a batch made early in the morning should be dry that same evening.

Sticks

As with cylinders, the ingredients for stick incense should all be in powder form. Use the ingredients and proportions called for in the recipes. Then add a little plain water and about a dozen drops of mineral oil. This makes the sticks much easier to work with and to form.

There are several methods for making stick incense. Among the more popular are the pre-made unscented, mold, dipping, and hand rolling methods.

The pre-made unscented method is by far the easiest to do. Just purchase pre-made unscented incense and add to them the essence or scent of your choice. The scent is "painted" on with a small artist's brush, then the stick is allowed to dry and stored until needed. If the scent is applied sparingly, the incense may be used right away. I'm a purist when it comes to incense, and don't really approve of this method. I must admit, however, that it comes in handy if you need a certain scent in a hurry and don't have the time to make it from scratch.

The mold method is very time consuming, but the finished product looks almost "store-bought." It consists of putting incense in a mold and pushing it back out as a finished stick of incense.

At a hobby shop, lumber or supply store, purchase a piece of metal tubing with an inside diameter of 1/4, 5/6, or 3/8 inch. A wooden dowel of the same diameter should also be obtained. Cut the tubing to a length of from 7 to 10 inches, and make the dowel about 4 inches longer than that. The tube will act as your mold, while the dowel will become the plunger. The dowel may need to be sanded to fit into the tube.

Knead the incense mixture like clay and put it into the mold. Pack it tightly with the plunger. Continue doing this until the tube is nearly full. Next, push a thin bamboo stick through one end, until it reaches the far end. With the dowel, gently push the stick and incense out of the mold.

Always clean the mold between blends and wash it when done. Before using the mold again, always soak it for a few minutes in warm water, just in case there may be some residue left inside from a previous batch.

The dipping method is not as time consuming as the mold method, but the sticks aren't as perfectly shaped either. In the dipping method, bamboo sticks are dipped into a solution of water, bonding agent, and saltpeter (if it is called for in the recipe). The sticks are then sprinkled with a powdered incense mixture and put aside for a few minutes to set up. After the incense has begun to harden (in about 15 minutes) the process is repeated. This will continue until the stick reaches the desired diameter, usually either 1/8 or 3/16 inch.

The solution must be changed between dippings because the fluid continues to thicken until it gets almost like gravy. If the sticks are dipped into a solution that is too thick, the solution can knock off the incense that is already on the stick.

Hand rolling is just what the name implies. The incense is placed on a smooth flat surface and rolled back and forth like you would a piece of clay or dough. When the desired thickness is reached, a bamboo stick is pushed through it, lengthwise, and it is shaped once more. Incense made by this method is very thick — usually from 3/8 to 1/2 inch in diameter. It is, however, easier and quicker than the previous two methods are.

You may be tempted to try your cake decorator to make stick incense, but it won't work. Any mixture that is moist enough to come out of the nozzle will be too wet to form stick incense.

You are probably wondering where to get bamboo sticks, since most occult shops and herb stores don't carry them. To overcome this problem, buy bamboo barbecue skewers and split them with a razor blade. Skewers usually come in packs of 100 and are not expensive. They can be obtained at any Oriental food store or at any store that sells outdoor cooking equipment.

Over the years, I've come across a number of blends that would not burn. In most cases, this problem can be corrected by replacing some of the non-combustible ingredients with their corresponding scents, oils or essences (see page 27). This will preserve the integrity of the blend, while also helping it burn more easily. If you do this, be sure to replace the missing bulk with a base, preferably one of either sandalwood or willow. If the blend still doesn't burn, don't get discouraged. The cone, cylinder, or stick can be ground with a mortar and pestle and used as a loose incense.

There are some recipes that don't burn independently. These are to be used as a loose incense only, and no bonding agent, liquid, or saltpeter is needed in them.

Unless otherwise stated, all recipes need 1/8 teaspoon of bonding agent (preferably tragacanth gum).

As far as liquid scents or oils go, use as much or little as you feel is needed. I usually use 10 drops of essence or 5 to 7 drops of oil, but, depending on personal tastes, or needs, anywhere from 5 to 20 drops will suffice.

DRYING AND STORING INCENSE

This section is devoted to drying and storing cone incense. The methods and techniques used can be readily adapted to the drying and storing of other types of incense as well. Proper drying is very important. Improperly dried incense takes much longer to dry and may even even be ruined.

Drying

When you have finished making the cones, place them in a vertical position for about an hour. This allows them to establish proper shape and symmetry. If this step is overlooked, the cones will tend to droop or lean toward one side.

The next step is to lay the cones flat, turning them occasionally. Lying them flat aids in drying, and when saltpeter is used, keeps it evenly distributed throughout the cone.

Wood is one of the best surfaces to dry incense on. It is economical, durable, and can be easily moved from place to place. It also absorbs excess moisture, thereby speeding up the drying process. Never use paper or cardboard for drying incense. Paper products soak up moisture too quickly, causing most of the saltpeter to be leached from the incense. A one-by-four or one-by-six inch board, cut about ten inches long, is about the right size for drying. It is small enough to sit on a windowsill or to be moved easily, yet large enough to hold several dozen incense cones. To keep the cones from rolling off the board, the outside edges should be either built up slightly or nails, brads, or push-pins can be driven in at half-inch intervals.

If you plan on drying stick incense, drill holes into the board about one inch apart. If you happen to be all thumbs, as I am, you can dry your sticks by poking them into a lump of clay, a block of styrofoam, or into a small can filled with sand.

In warm weather, cones can be easily dried on a windowsill or in the back window of an automobile. It usually takes about two days for them to dry in a window, and about a day and a half to dry in the sun in a car.

Several things can adversely effect the drying of incense. Among these are dew, high humidity, shade, improper ventilation, and cold. Any one of these conditions can severely retard drying or even ruin your incense. Remember, when you dry incense outdoors or in a car, you must bring it indoors at night. This precaution will help to eliminate the possibility of your incense being ruined by dew.

Incense dries very slowly when the humidity is high or on rainy days. Always check the weather forecast before making incense. Postpone making incense if the forecast calls for two or more days of adverse weather. Incense needs direct sunlight and/ or heat to dry quickly and completely. If left in a shady or cool spot, it will take much longer to dry.

Proper ventilation is a must when drying incense. It should never be covered or placed in a box to dry. This will greatly lengthen drying time and increase the possibility of the incense being ruined by mildew.

During cold weather, always dry incense indoors. It can be easily dried on a sunny windowsill, or near a heater vent. Depending upon the heat used, it will take from one to three days to dry.

How do you tell when your cones are dry? Simply squeeze them between your thumb and forefinger, at their base. Press gently at first, then increase the pressure. The cones are dry if you can squeeze them as hard as you can and they neither give way nor break. This method only works when using tragacanth gum as a bonding agent. Cones made of gum arabic (or almost any other gum) will be too fragile to be tested in this way.

Don't be impatient. The drying times given here are only approximate. Weather conditions, ingredients used, and the quality and freshness of the herbs used all have an effect on the drying time. Incense dries from the outside inward. It may appear dry while the inside may still be quite damp. (The fresher the herb, the longer it takes to dry.)

Storing

After your incense is completely dry, it should be carefully stored for future use. I cannot emphasize enough the need for proper storage. All of your work will have been in vain if your incense is stored haphazardly.

Each blend should be stored separately. Loose incense can be stored in small wide-mouthed jars, for easy retrieval. Cones and cylinders can be stored in jars or tightly sealed plastic bags. Stick incense should be placed in a tall thin jar, such as an empty catsup or soft drink bottle.

Remember to label the containers. Record the ingredients or recipe, date made, and any other fact that you think may be important. It is very easy to forget or get confused if your blends are left unmarked.

When you make larger batches, or use liquid scents or strong scents (such as camphor or menthol), glass must always be used for storage. If possible, add a small packet of silica gel to guard against moisture.

Store all incense in a dark dry place, well out of the reach of children and pets. The darkness will help to preserve the color and potency of the incense. The dryness will aid in the prevention of moisture build-up and mildew. The safest and best storage locations that I've found are on the top shelves of closets and in overhead kitchen cabinets.

ADDING COLOR

If you wish to make colored incense, it is best to use liquid coloring. The color is first mixed with your liquid solution, and then added to the dry ingredients.

Candle coloring makes a good dye, but the easiest, cheapest, and most practical coloring to use is food coloring. It can be obtained in almost any supermarket, and because it's inorganic, it's stable and will last indefinitely.

Coloring works best with a base and scent mixture, rather than with an herbal blend. An all-base incense takes color easily because it's very light in color to begin with. On the other hand, herbal blends are much darker in color, usually green or brown. Dark colors resist coloring to the extent that the best you can expect is a tint of the desired color.

Coloring will increase burning time. If too much color is used, it can adversely effect the combustibility of an incense.

Unless you can obtain other pre-mixed colors, it is best to stay with the basic colors of yellow, red, blue, and green. No incense is light enough in color to be dyed with a blend of shades.

If you are coloring a base and scent mixture, use 6 drops of dye for cones and cylinders, and 5 drops for stick incense. For herbal blends, use 1 drop of coloring for every 1/2 teaspoon of dry ingredients used. Always wear rubber gloves when working with coloring. If you get any on your hands, it's hard to get off.

When making more than one color at a time, make sure to dry the different colors separately. If different colors are allowed to touch while drying, they will run together.

If you prefer natural coloring, you can use an herb or base that supplies the color you desire. For example, Red Sandalwood for red, Willow for brown, Safflower for yellow, and Willow

Charcoal for black. When adding extra ingredients for coloring, be sure to adjust the recipe accordingly.

Many practitioners of the occult sciences use color in conjunction with magic. Each color is believed to have dominion over a certain aspect of life. The combination of appropriate herbs and color is thought to greatly enhance the power of magical spells and workings.

The following is an abbreviated list of some of the alleged magical influences of the ten most common colors. It is not all inclusive, and is only meant to show the vast spheres of influence that color is thought to control.

Black: banishes illness and negative feelings, breaks spells, brings about release or ends negative situations; used in exorcisms.

Blue: increases concentration; calms emotions; strengthens friendships, honesty; protects secrets; increases knowledge, love, loyalty, marriage, meditation, peace, perseverance, psychic development and growth; protection from harm; spirituality; stops gossip, aids in studying, creates tranquility, increases wisdom.

Brown: working with and healing of animals; enhances domestic tranquility; brings an increase of material objects (when used with green); causes neutrality.

Green: abundance and increase; to bring a thing into being; to increase confidence, energy, fertility, gain, growth; bring good luck, hope, money, peace; aids in the nurturing of plants; prosperity; increase of psychic development and growth; renewal, success, tranquility; attracts wealth.

Orange: enhances adaptability; causes attraction; increases concentration; builds confidence, endurance, energy, fulfillment; brings about inspiration; aids meditation; attracts prosperity; helps psychic development and growth, satisfaction, thought.

Pink: increases affection; causes fidelity; brings friendship; attracts true love.

Purple: increases ambition; brings authority, business and trade, determination; divine intervention; to increase or enhance occult powers, law, magic; overcome opposition; protection from harm; success.

Red: increases courage and strength; renews energy, intellect; helps obtain material objects; overcome opposition; passion, power, sex, increases wealth.

White: brings about awareness and understanding; for all general magical workings; brings about happiness, honesty, loyalty, peace; protection (physical and psychic); purification, religion and spirituality; tranquility.

Yellow: attraction; aids in career; brings about change; confidence, devotion, happiness; brings inspiration; increases knowledge, peace and tranquility; protects the traveler; wisdom.

USING LIQUID SCENTS

Oils and scents greatly enhance the incense you make in terms of fragrance. They also help eliminate most nonburning recipes because you can replace poor burning herbs with their corresponding scents and an easily combustible base. If you replace an herb with its scent, the recipe will stay the same. The bulk is replaced by a base. For example, if you replace 1/2 teaspoon of herb with scent, you must add 1/2 teaspoon of base.

Most herbs are also sold in liquid scents. There are four basic types of liquid scents: essential oil (sometimes called essence), extract, tincture, and artificial. The best is essential oil. The aroma of an herb can be greatly enhanced by adding a few drops of its liquid scent to it.

When buying scents, it pays to shop around. Some retailers sell pure essence, while others sell it cut or even artificially reproduced. If you are unsure about a particular retailer's goods, ask people who may have done business with the retailer before. Price is another factor to consider when buying scents. A high-priced product may not always be stronger or of better quality. There's no way to tell a scent's quality by price alone.

Always try before you buy. If you order by mail, buy just one bottle of the smallest size available. If it meets with your approval, then the next time you can buy more and in a larger size. If it doesn't please you, then you've not lost too much.

Liquid scents should be stored in dark glass containers. If they come in clear glass, they should be stored in a dark place. This will help to preserve freshness and strength.

Never store scents in a plastic container, as the plastic will "bleed" into the scent. This will make the incense smell like melted plastic when it is burned.

Scents should never be exposed to direct sunlight for extended periods of time. Sunlight weakens the scent and, if it has been cut with an organic substance, can turn it rancid.

In time, even the highest quality scents will loose their potency. To help combat this, buy scents in small amounts, and replenish your supply often.

When working with scents, wear rubber gloves if possible. Unprotected skin may be irritated by some scents. This is particularly true if you are susceptible to rashes and other skin problems. If you don't wear gloves, your hands will become impregnated with scent. To remove the smell, wash your hands thoroughly with soap and water. Then wash them in a mixture of 1 cup water and 1 tablespoon of lemon juice. Next, wash again with soap and water.

If you have a fresh lemon, rub a slice of it over your hands to remove unwanted scents. If you have neither lemon juice nor fresh lemons, then straight tomato juice will help (although not as well).

After you have made your incense, it should be stored separately. If you don't, the scents will run into each other, making all the different blends have a similar fragrance.

My recipes call for oil, also known as essential oil, scent, or essence. Tincture and extract may also be used, although they aren't as strong or long lasting.

Essential oils are usually cut with almond, sunflower, olive, or mineral oils. Tinctures, extracts, and most artificial scents are cut with alcohol. This makes them fairly easy to tell apart. If a scent feels slightly oily to the touch, it is probably an essential oil. If it feels cool and watery, it is a tincture, extract, or an artificial scent.

The strength of a scent depends mostly on the manufacturer and the type of herb used. A rough estimate of the different types of scents is as follows. A tincture, being made up of mostly alcohol, is only about half as strong as its corresponding herb. An extract is approximately four times stronger than the fresh herb. Essential oil can be anywhere from five to ten times more powerful than the herb. Artificially produced scents fall somewhere between extracts and essential oils in strength.

If you are using only scent and a base, a good formula to use is: 2 teaspoons Sandalwood, 1/2 teaspoon talc (or baby powder), 1/8 teaspoon tragacanth, 5 drops mineral oil, 10 to 15 drops essential oil, and 2 teaspoons water. This recipe will make about 5 cones, which will burn approximately fifteen minutes each.

The recipe for stick incense is: 2 teaspoons Sandalwood, 2 teaspoons water, 8 drops mineral oil, 1/8 teaspoon tragacanth, and 7 to 10 drops scent. This will be enough to make one hand-rolled stick. The stick will be about 6 1/2 inches long, 7/16 inch diameter, and will burn about an hour and a half.

The strengths of various scents vary so much that it is often difficult to know how much fragrance to use when replacing a particular herb. A rough estimate is about five drops of essential oil for every 1/2 teaspoon of herb that is replaced. This is only an approximation, and there are numerous exceptions.

When using scents, the incense must be dried and stored as quickly as possible. The longer the incense takes to dry, the more scent will be lost. If too much scent has been lost in drying, it can be replaced by "painting" more on. Just before the incense is to be used, scent may be added with a small paint brush. The scent should be applied sparingly, or the incense may become too damp to burn properly.

The following are four nice blends of scent[1] that you might like to try. They can be used either as a scent for incense or applied as a perfume.

Mystic

1/2 oz. Mineral Oil	13 drops Rose Geranium Oil
13 drops Myrrh Oil	1/4 tsp. High John (Jalap) Oil

Shake daily for seven days before using.

---

[1] All four recipes are courtesy of Ellen Hansen, and are reprinted by permission.

Isis

1 oz. Mineral Oil	6 drops Bay Oil
6 drops Bayberry Oil	8 drops Benzoin Oil
4 drops Frankincense Oil	4 drops Rose Oil
4 drops Sandalwood Oil	

Let sit for two weeks before using.

Love

1/2 oz. Mineral Oil	6 drops Orris Oil
2 drops Rose Oil	2 drops Musk Oil
2 drops Strawberry Oil	

Let sit one week before using

Uncrossing

1/2 oz. Mineral Oil	12 drops Maguet or Coconut Oil
1 pinch powdered Sandalwood	
1 pinch powdered Dragon's Blood	

Shake daily for seven days before using.

HOW TO BURN INCENSE

Whether you call them censers, thuribles, or just plain incense burners, they are all the same thing—something in which to burn incense. You can obtain incense burners in an almost unlimited variety of styles and sizes. You can even make your own. If you choose to make your own, you can make an incense burner from anything from a coffee or tuna can to a crystal goblet, from a paper milk carton to a fancy ceramic bowl. The choice and style of the burner is entirely up to you after you consider which type of incense you want to burn.

There are some things that all incense burners have in common. They should be designed and built so they will prevent the heat of burning incense and/or charcoal from spreading and causing a possible fire. They should also be made so that there is a good flow of air around the incense. If you use either loose incense or cones, the burner should have a small wire screen or a layer of small pebbles underneath the incense. This will insure a good flow of air around the incense. Without this flow, charcoal won't burn properly and cone incense will not burn completely.

When burning cylinder or stick incense, your burner should be filled with fine-grained sand. Sand from the seashore is best, but any clean sand from a riverbed or stream will do. Sand is used for many reasons—it is easy to keep clean, it's inexpensive to use or replace, and if it is added to a crystal bowl or fancy censer, it adds a natural beauty.

Using Charcoal

Loose incense is usually burned on charcoal briquettes. The charcoal used is not your everyday barbecue charcoal; it is a blend that is specially designed for use with incense. It is less toxic, uses more exotic ingredients, and is easier to light than its backyard cousin. Most charcoal briquettes used for incense are imported and expensive. If you don't mind a little mess, you can make your own for less than half the price. The recipes for homemade charcoal briquettes won't light as quickly or easily as the store-bought variety, but they will burn for nearly as long. Best of all, they will be made by you.

Recipe #1 Sweet Charcoal

Willow charcoal 5   Benzoin $1/4$
Sandalwood 1   Tragacanth $1/4$
Saltpeter $1/8$ Water 5

This blend has a slightly sweet, flowery, and woody scent when burned.

Recipe #2 Unscented

Willow charcoal 6   Sandalwood $1/2$
Tragacanth $1/4$ Saltpeter $1/8$
Water 5

This blend has almost no scent at all.

To make these recipes, combine the water and saltpeter; mix occasionally until the saltpeter is thoroughly dissolved. Next, mix all the dry ingredients together, then add the liquid and mix again.

When your mixture has been thoroughly mixed, put it into a mold. The recipes given will make two or three briquettes, depending on the size of the mold.

The molds can be homemade and can be either permanent or disposable. Permanent molds can be made by cutting empty stick deodorant tubes into rings that are $7/16$ or $1/2$ inch high. Disposable molds are easily fashioned from empty paper towel or bathroom tissue rolls, and cut into rings.

After you have packed the mixture into the molds, a round depression should be put onto the top of each. This depression will act as a kind of bowl, to hold the burning incense. The depression is made by gently pushing a round object into the mixture, twisting it, then removing it. A ping-pong ball or the ball from a roll-on deodorant works nicely.

Charcoal shrinks when it dries, because of the large amount of water used. This makes it easy to remove from the molds when it is dry.

Always dry your charcoal on foil. This will prevent the saltpeter from being leached away.

To light your charcoal, hold an edge of it over a lit candle until you are sure that it is lit. Do the same thing to one or two other "corners." Be careful not to burn yourself. Put the lit charcoal into a censer and wait a minute or two to make sure that it is lit. Then use and enjoy the product of your labor.

Part
Two

HERBAL

GATHERING, DRYING, AND STORING HERBS

There are some basic steps to follow when gathering, drying, and storing your own herbs. Should you desire more detailed methods, your local library should have several books on drying plants and herbs.

The best time to gather herbs is just before they flower. It is at this time that they are at their peak of strength and growth. Herbs should be harvested in the morning, just after the dew has evaporated and before the sun gets too hot. Picking too early can cause them to mildew, rot, or develop spots. Picking too late will cause them to burn and lose much of their color and potency.

When picking leaves, flowers, etc., always cut them from the plant, never tear or rip them off. Tearing can damage or kill a plant. After all, you just want to use some of its folage, not destroy it. All living things should be treated with respect.

Cleanliness is a must when drying and storing herbs. Before they are to be dried, herbs should be soaked in clean water, and then patted dry. This will remove any dust, dirt, or insects that may be on them.

All herbs should be dried away from direct sunlight. Direct exposure to the sun will cause the herbs to lose most of their color and potency. On the other hand, drying herbs in a shady or dark place will help preserve both.

Branches, large leaves, or whole plants, should be tied in small bunches and hung upside down to dry. If you are cramped for space, they may be hung from a coat hanger in a closet.

If you dry your bunches in a garage, shed, or attic, always cover them with a paper bag. The bag will keep them safe from dust and insects. Never use plastic bags, as they retain the moisture that evaporates from the plants.

Depending on weather conditions and the type of plant being dried, bunches will usually take from one to three weeks to dry. A bunch is dry when you can crumble its leaves to powder between your fingers and the stems break with a loud snap.

Leaves and flower petals should be spread out to dry on a screen or tray. Use only whole leaves or petals. Discard all spotted, decayed, or insect eaten ones.

For best results, leaves and flower petals should be dried indoors away from direct sunlight. It usually takes from three to five days for them to dry thoroughly. They are dry if they crumble or make a crackling sound when squeezed.

Roots should first be washed in clean water and then patted dry. Small roots should be cut in half lengthwise. Roots ½ inch or larger should be quartered. Roots should then be put on a screen or tray to dry, and turned daily. Most roots will take from two to five weeks to dry. Dried roots will break with a loud snap when broken in two.

Always pick seeds or seed pods on a warm sunny day. Use only ripe seeds or brown (or grey) seed pods. Most seeds will take from three to fourteen days to dry, depending on their size. Dry seeds will break with a snap when cut in two with a knife.

If you lack adequate space for drying, you can dry your herbs on an aluminum or foil pie plate. Each plate can hold three or four layers of herbs if they are spread thinly and you put a piece of tissue paper between each layer.

Small paper bags are another space saver. Place your herbs loosely inside and close the bag. Shake the bag two or three times daily so that the herbs will dry evenly. A sealed bag will protect both the color and potency of herbs. Bags may also be placed in direct sunlight, thereby greatly reducing drying time. Check your herbs occasionally to make sure they haven't been "cooked" by too much heat.

In warm weather, an automobile makes an excellent place to dry herbs. Place the herbs on a pie plate or in a paper bag on the *floor* of the vehicle. On a warm day, with the windows open about one inch, the temperature can rise to over 100 degrees inside a car. With the windows completely closed, it can rise to at least

140 degrees! Don't put leaves of flowers in direct sunlight as they will spoil from too much heat. In my opinion, herbs placed in a paper bag and dried inside an automobile is by far the best method of drying. The herbs dry very quickly and yet retain their color, potency, and fragrance. They are also protected from dust, insects, and accidental spillage.

When drying herbs in a car, or anywhere outdoors, be sure to bring them indoors at night. Failure to do so could expose your herbs to dew buildup. Moisture on herbs or even on drying bags will increase drying time and can even cause them to be ruined by rot or mildew.

After your herbs are thoroughly dry, they should be ground as finely as possible. When ground to a powder-like consistency, the herbs are easier to work with.

Most herbs, such as leaves, flower petals, and small seeds can be easily ground in a blender. Place about one cup of dried herbs in your blender and run it at low speed for about a minute. For harder substances, such as roots, bark, or wood, a coffee grinder or a mortar and pestle should be used.

When you have finished grinding your herbs, sift them to remove any lumps or unground pieces. A window screen or a hand-held flour sifter can be used for this purpose.

Always store your herbs in glass or ceramic containers. These help preserve freshness, color, and potency. Opaque or translucent containers are best, although clear glass can be used if it is stored in a dark dry place.

Never store your herbs in a plastic container. The plastic will "bleed" into the herbs, causing them to give off a plastic-like scent when burned.

Storage containers and drying equipment should always be washed and carefully dried before use. These precautions should be followed at all times to help prevent contamination and spoilage.

For economy minded people, empty jelly jars or pint sized canning jars are excellent for storing herbs. A jelly jar that held 18 ounces of jelly will hold about four ounces of herbs. A one pint mason jar will hold approximately five ounces of powdered herbs.

Herbs should be stored in a dark dry place. The top shelf of a closet or an overhead cabinet is best. This will not only protect your herbs, but keeps them away from inquisitive children and pets. Stored herbs should be checked occasionally for signs of mildew or mold. It will usually appear as either little fluffy balls on the surface of the herbs, or as a stringy mass that holds small clumps of your herb together. If this should occur, re-sift and re-dry your herbs immediately.

The best way to re-dry herbs is to put them in a pie plate and place them in your oven. Set the oven at its lowest temperature and heat the herbs for one or two hours. Check them occasionally to make sure that they don't burn or turn brown. If you don't want to be stuck in the kitchen "baby-sitting" your herbs, use your oven light and no heat. The light alone will give off enough heat to dry the herbs overnight.

If your herbs become moldly or mildewed a second time, throw them out. Be sure to also re-wash the container thoroughly before using it again.

If properly dried and stored, most herbs will last for two or three years without loosing too much of their strength. It is, however, better to replace them yearly. This will insure that your herbs are always fresh and fragrant.

HERBAL

This herbal is an alphabetical listing of the most common herbs used when making incense. Each listing includes useful information about each herb: the herb's most commonly used name, its Latin name, the part of the herb used for making incense, the ruling planet and element, a list of its alleged magical uses, comments about the herb's scent, and a recipe for using the herb to make incense. I have also included general information, or notes, at the end of the listing if I had it to share with you, or if I thought it was important.

To save space, the recipes have been consolidated, so you will see only a list of measures following the recipe heading. These numbers should be read from left to right. The first number refers to the amount of herb (or essence) to be used, then the base, the gum (preferably tragacanth), and the liquid needed for the bonding agent. All measurements are in teaspoons, or fractions thereof. If you want to increase or decrease the recipe, see Appendices 2 and 3 at the back of this book for instructions. If you don't remember how to make the bonding agent, please refer to QB, LF, and FW on page 14.

The magical uses listing in the herbal are brief, and are meant to be keywords for magical uses. These same keywords are used in the recipes sections of this book. For a more detailed explanation of what each keyword really refers to in terms of magical use, see Appendix 6 on page 267. I would like to point out that these are alleged magical uses; I make no claim, one way or the other, as to their validity. Also, no negative or harmful uses have been included in the magical uses section. All forms of life are sacred and should always be treated with honor and respect. When you come across a magical use that lists "Animals," this means that the herb listed is believed to be beneficial to animals and/or animal owners; for example, for healing animals or to aid in training of animals.

Some of the following herbs list only essence for the part used and give no recipe. This is because the herbs themselves are unsuitable for the making of incense, but their scents are used. Many flowers fall into this category. Fresh flowers smell wonderful — most dried ones have no floral scent at all. When an essence is mentioned in *part used*, it means essential oil. Artificial scents, extracts, and tinctures should be used only if essential oil is not obtainable.

I've left the use of oils in the blends up the the individual. Usually 5 to 10 drops is enough. With oils, not enough is better than too much. You can always add more, but you can't take any away.

When you come across a recipeless herb listing, use the following basic formula: a base of 2½ teaspoons Sandalwood, ⅛ teaspoon Tragacanth, and 1¾ teaspoons of water. Scent can be used at the time of making the incense or applied just prior to use.

Acacia
Acacia Senegal

Common names:	Cape Gum, Egyptian Thorn, Gum Arabic, Hachah
Part used:	Flowers, Essence
Planet:	Sun
Element:	Fire
Magical uses:	Contact with other planes, gain, harmony, increase the power of spells, insure agreements and pacts, meditation, attract money, peace, protection, psychic development & growth, tranquility.
Recipe:	2$^1/_2$, 1, $^1/_8$, 1$^1/_4$, FW
Scent:	Strong, grassy, bittersweet

Dried acacia flowers are relatively harmless; however, care should be taken when using essence. Acacia oil can cause allergic reactions such as skin rashes, hay fever, or asthma attacks. If taken internally, it can cause serious gastro-intestinal disorders. Acacia flowers are sometimes adulterated, or even replaced, with locust flowers. Their scents are very similar, but their colors are slightly different. Acacia is brownish-yellow, while locust flowers are more yellow than brown.

Agar Agar
Gelidium Amansii

Common name:	Japanese Isinglass
Part used:	Mucilage
Planet:	Moon
Element:	Water
Magical uses:	In times past, it was used in rites involving the sea.
Scent:	Salty, marsh-like
Recipe:	Loose only

Agar agar is no longer widely used for incense, except occasionally as a bonding agent.

Agrimony
Agrimonia Eupatoria

Common names:	Church Steeples, Cockleburr, Garclive, Philanthropos, Sticklewort
Part used:	Leaves and Stems
Planet:	Jupiter
Element:	Fire
Magical uses:	Gain, good luck, keep secrets, material objects, money, prosperity, protection, psychic protection, retention, wealth
Recipe:	$2^1/_2$, $^1/_4$, $^1/_8$, 2, Water
Scent:	Mild, dry, grassy, bitter

Allspice
Pimenta Officinalis

Common names:	Jamaica Pepper, Pimento
Part used:	Fruit, essence
Planet:	Venus
Element:	Earth
Magical uses:	Compassion, determination, fertility, gain, love, renewal
Recipe:	$2^1/_2$, $^1/_4$, $^1/_8$, $1^1/_2$ Water
Scent:	Warm, spicy, semi-sweet, mild

Almond
Amygdalus communis

Common names:	Greek Nuts, Shakad
Part used:	Essence
Planet:	Venus
Element:	Air
Magical uses:	Aphrodisiac, compassion, fertility, love, material objects, money, prosperity, wealth
Scent:	Rich, sweet, fruity, flowery
Recipe:	Oil applied to a base of Sandalwood

Aloe
Aloe Vera

Common names:	Bitter Aloes, Cape Aloes, Shoot of Paradise
Part used:	Leaves
Planet:	Moon
Element:	Water
Magical uses:	Gain, renewal, strength
Recipe:	Loose only
Scent:	Semi-sweet, powerful, unearthly

Do not confuse aloes with lignum aloes. The aloes we will use are common houseplants many people use for minor cuts and burns. Lignum aloes are hard to obtain, very expensive, and too overated to be of any real use.

Althea
Althaea Officinalis

Common names:	Marsh Mallow, Mortification Root, Sweet Weed, Wymote
Part used:	Leaves
Planet:	Venus
Element:	Earth
Magical uses:	Clairvoyance, contact other planes, determination, divination, harmony, peace, psychic development & growth, tranquility
Recipe:	2$^1/_2$, $^1/_4$, $^1/_8$, 1$^1/_2$ Water
Scent:	Tart, bitter, green, fishy

Ambergris
Latin name: None

Part used:	Essence (use artificial)
Planet:	Venus
Element:	Earth
Magical uses:	Animals, aphrodisiac, commanding, increases power of spells, love, passion, sensuality, virility
Scent:	Intense, sweet, old-fashioned, flowery

Genuine ambergris comes from the intestinal tract of the Sperm Whale. I strongly recommend that you use only artificially produced essence. No animal should have to give up its life to satisfy the cosmetic whims of humans.

Angelica
Angelica Archangelica

Common names:	Archangel, Masterwort
Part used:	Root, essence
Planet:	Sun
Element:	Fire
Magical uses:	Contact other planes, divine intervention, exorcism, gain, inspiration, knowledge, love, magic, protection, psychic protection, renewal, spell-breaking, success, wisdom
Recipe:	Loose only
Scent:	Bitter light, tart

Care should be taken when handling angelica oil. When exposed to sunlight, it can cause the skin to swell or may form a rash.

Anise
Pimpinella Anisium

Common name:	Aniseed
Part used:	Seed, essence
Planet:	Mercury
Element:	Air
Magical uses:	Aphrodisiac, clairvoyance, consecration, contact other planes, divination, fertility, gain, good luck, love, money, prevent nightmares, protection, psychic development & growth, psychic protection
Recipe:	Loose only
Scent:	Bittersweet, nutty, spicy, full-bodied

Asafoetida
Ferula Foetida

Common names:	Devil's Dung, Ferula, Food of the Gods
Part used:	Gum
Planet:	Saturn
Element:	Earth
Magical uses:	Consecration, endings, exorcism, overcome opposition, protection, psychic protection, release, spell-breaking
Recipe:	$1/2$, 2, $1/8$, $1^3/4$, QB
Scent:	Overpowering, rotten meat, dung

The old grimores relied heavily on asafoetida as an ingredient in spells of exorcism and black magic. Its smell is so offensive, however, that its use has been almost eliminated in recent years.

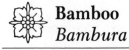 **Balm of Gilead**
Populus Candicans

Common names:	Balm Mint, Mecca Balsam, Poplar Buds
Part used:	Buds, essence
Planet:	Jupiter
Element:	Fire
Magical uses:	Inspiration, knowledge, love, protection, strength, virility, wisdom
Recipe:	1¹/₂, 1¹/₂, ¹/₈, 1³/₄, FW
Scent:	Intense, bittersweet, resin-like

Bamboo
Bambura

Common name:	Bamba Wood, Tae
Part used:	Wood
Planet:	Moon
Element:	Water
Recipe:	2¹/₂, 0, ¹/₈, 1¹/₂ QB
Scent:	Sweet, grassy, woody

Basil
Ocimum Basilicum

Common names:	Alabahaca, American Dittany, Herb of Kings, St. Josephswort, Tulsi, Witches' Herb
Part used:	Leaves and stems, essence
Planet:	Mars
Element:	Fire
Magical uses:	Aphrodisiac, brighten disposition, clairvoyance, commanding, consecration, divination, exorcism, fertility, fidelity, happiness, harmony, honesty, love, material objects, money, passion, peace, prosperity, protection, psychic development & growth, psychic protection, spell-breaking, strength, success, tranquility, wealth
Recipe:	2$^1/_2$, $^1/_2$, $^1/_8$, 1$^1/_2$, FW
Scent:	Bittersweet, herby, mild

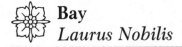 **Bay**
Laurus Nobilis

Common names:	Daphne, Laurel
Part used:	Leaves, essence
Planet:	Sun
Element:	Fire
Magical uses:	Aphrodisiac, clairvoyance, consecration, divination, endings, exorcism, good luck, harmony, inspiration, knowledge, love, magic, memory, money, overcome opposition, peace, protection, psychic development & growth, psychic protection, release, spell-breaking, tranquility, transformation, wisdom
Recipe:	$2^{1}/_{2}$, $^{1}/_{4}$, $^{1}/_{8}$, $1^{3}/_{4}$ QB
Scent:	Herby, dreamy, mysterious, hint of mint

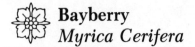

Bayberry
Myrica Cerifera

Common name:	Wax Myrtle
Part used:	Bark of root, essence
Planet:	Mercury
Element:	Earth
Magical uses:	Domestic tranquility, good luck, harmony, material objects, money, peace, prosperity, tranquility, wealth, well-being
Recipe:	$2^1/_2$, $^1/_4$, $^1/_8$, $2^1/_4$ QB
Scent:	Mild, sweet, woody

Bayberry bark doesn't smell as strong or pleasing as a bayberry candle would. To get that kind of scent you must use its essence. If using essence, care should be taken as it can cause minor skin irritation.

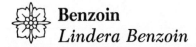

Benzoin
Lindera Benzoin

Common names:	Benjamin, Friar's Balsam, Spice Bush, Sumatra Gum
Part used:	Gum, essence
Planet:	Venus
Element:	Air
Magical uses:	Exorcism, harmony, inspiration, knowledge, love, memory, peace, peace of mind, protection, psychic protection, spell-breaking, tranquility, wisdom
Recipe:	$^1/_2$, 2, $^1/_8$, $1^1/_2$ Water
Scent:	Sweet, flowery, perfume-like

Essence of benzoin may cause minor allergic reactions in some people.

Bergamot
Monarda Fistulosa / Citrus Bergamia

Common names:	Bee Balm, Monarda, Mountain Balm, Mountain Mint, Oswego Tea, Scarlet Monarda
Part used:	Essence
Planet:	Sun
Element:	Fire
Magical uses:	Aphrodisiac, love, material objects, prosperity, protection, sensuality, strength, success, wealth
Scent:	Rich, full-bodied, flowery, citrus-like

When exposed to direct sunlight, bergamot essence can cause the skin to spot.

Bindweed
Convolvulus Avensis

Common name:	Creeping Jenny
Part used:	Root
Planet:	Saturn
Element:	Earth
Magical uses:	Gambling, good luck, law, love, material objects, money, prosperity, protection, wealth
Recipe:	$2^1/_2$, $^1/_4$, $^1/_8$, $1^1/_2$ QB
Scent:	Tart, green, bitter

Bindweed is sometimes used as an adulterant for Jalap Root and Scammony Root. Although it is in the same family as both, it is nowhere near as pleasant or powerful as either one.

Black Haw
Viburnum Prunifolium

Common name:	Haw
Part used:	Root
Planet:	Mercury
Element:	Air
Magical uses:	Contact other planes, weather
Recipe:	3, 0, 1/8, 1 3/4 Water
Scent:	Gentle, sweet, woody

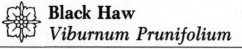 **Blueberry**
Vaccinium Corymbosum

Common name:	None
Part used:	Leaves, essence
Planet:	Venus
Element:	Earth
Magical uses:	Fertility, gain
Recipe:	2 1/2, 1/4, 1/8, 1 3/4 QB
Scent:	Bittersweet, herby, gentle

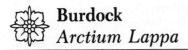

Broom
Cytisus Scoparius

Common names:	Asphaltus, Banal, Bealadh, Besom, Genista, Link
Part used:	Tops of plant
Planet:	Mars
Element:	Fire
Magical uses:	Compassion, consecration, exorcism, magic, modesty, passion, protection, psychic protection, raising & calming winds, spell-breaking, weather, weddings
Recipe:	Loose only
Scent:	Bittersweet, grassy, slightly tart

Burdock
Arctium Lappa

Common names:	Bardana, Bat Weed, Beggar's Buttons, Cockleburr, Fox's Clote, Hardock, Lappa, Love Leaves, Personata
Parts used:	Root
Planet:	Venus
Element:	Earth
Magical uses:	Animals, compassion, consecration, exorcism, love, protection, spell-breaking
Recipe:	2¹/₂, ¹/₂, ¹/₈, 2 FW
Scent:	Subtle, tart, bitter

Calamus
Acorus Calamus

Common names:	Acoron, Costus, Gladdon, Sedge, Sweet Flag, Sweet Sedge
Part used:	Root
Planet:	Venus
Element:	Earth
Magical uses:	Aphrodisiac, commanding, harmony, love, peace, tranquility
Recipe:	2½, ¼, ⅛, 2 Water
Scent:	Arid, mild, floral, mysterious

Camomile
Anthemis Nobilis/ Matricaria Chamomilla

Common names:	Chamomile, Ground Apple, Kamai Melon, Manzanilla, Maythen
Part used:	Flowers, essence
Planet:	Sun
Element:	Fire
Magical uses:	Beauty, determination, dreams, gentleness, good luck, harmony, material objects, meditation, modesty, money, peace, tranquility, wealth
Recipe:	Loose only
Scent:	Bittersweet, herby, hint of apple

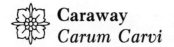 Camphor
Cinnamonum Camphora

Common name:	None
Part used:	Gum, essence
Planet:	Moon
Element:	Water
Magical uses:	Break off an affair, endings, psychic development & growth, release
Recipe:	1/2, 2 1/2, 1/8, 2 Water
Scent:	Strong, penetrating, cool

Most camphor used today is artificially produced by combining hydrogen-chloride gas and oil of turpentine. It is highly toxic and should be handled and stored carefully. Swallowing even a small amount will cause dizziness, unconsciousness, or even death.

Caraway
Carum Carvi

Common name:	Kummel
Part used:	Seeds, essence
Planet:	Mercury
Element:	Air
Magical uses:	Aphrodisiac, fertility, fidelity, gain, honesty, keep secrets, love, memory, passion, peace of mind, prevents theft, protection, retention, sensuality
Recipe:	2, 1, 1/8, 1 1/2 LF
Scent:	Full-bodied, nutty, bittersweet

To get the distinctive aroma of fresh caraway, you must use oil. If you do, handle it carefully, as it can cause allergic reactions or skin irritation.

Cascara Sagrada
Rhamus Purshiana

Common names:	Buckthorn, Chittem Bark, Sacred Bark
Part used:	Bark
Planet:	Saturn
Element:	Earth
Magical uses:	Consecration, contact other planes, exorcism, good luck, law, money, protection, spell-breaking
Recipe:	$2^{1}/_{2}$, $1/_{4}$, $1/_{8}$, 2 QB
Scent:	Bittersweet, woody, mysterious

Cascarilla
Croton Eleuteria

Common name:	Sweet Bark
Part used:	Bark
Planet:	Mars
Element:	Fire
Magical uses:	Harmony, peace, rites involving males, sensuality, tranquility, virility
Recipe:	3, 0, $1/_{8}$, 2 Water
Scent:	Woody, semi-sweet, fiery yet delicate

Cassia
Cinnamonum Cassia

Common names:	Chinese Cinnamon, Senna, Sweet Wood
Part used:	Bark, essence
Planet:	Mercury
Element:	Air
Magical uses:	Aphrodisiac, clairvoyance, consecration, divination, good luck, harmony, increase the power of spells, inspiration, knowledge, love, material objects, meditation, money, passion, peace, prosperity, protection, psychic development & growth, tranquility, wealth, wisdom
Recipe:	2¹/₂, ¹/₂, ¹/₈, 2¹/₄ QB
Scent:	Warm, sweet, spicy

Cassia is a member of the cinnamon family and is widely used as a substitute for cinnamon. There is almost no difference in either taste or smell. Since cassia comes from mainland China, it's cheaper to use. In fact, the "cinnamon" in your spice rack is probably cassia!

Catnip
Nepeta Cataria

Common names:	Catmint, Field Balm, Nip
Part used:	Leaves
Planet:	Venus
Element:	Air
Magical uses:	Animals, commanding, dreams, harmony, love, peace, rest, sleep, tranquility
Recipe:	2¹/₂, ¹/₄, ¹/₈, 2 Water
Scent:	Herby, grassy, hint of minty tartness

Cedar
Cedrus

Common names:	Green Incense, Sandarac, Tree of Life
Part used:	Foliage, essence
Planet:	Jupiter
Element:	Fire
Magical uses:	Clairvoyance, consecration, divination, gain, longevity, material objects, prosperity, strength, success, wealth
Recipe:	$2^{1}/_{2}$, 0, $^{1}/_{8}$, $1^{1}/_{4}$ FW
Scent:	Woody, evergreen, robust

Cedar essence can cause allergic reactions to people with delicate skin, particularly if exposed to direct sunlight.

Celery
Apium Graveolens

Common name:	Minari, Han-ch'in
Part used:	Seed, essence
Planet:	Saturn
Element:	Earth
Magical uses:	Aphrodisiac, beauty, fertility, love, psychic development & growth
Recipe:	$1^{1}/_{2}$, 1, $^{1}/_{8}$, $1^{1}/_{4}$ LF
Scent:	Bittersweet, herby, celery-like

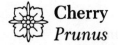

Cherry
Prunus

Common name:	None
Part used:	Bark, essence
Planet:	Venus
Element:	Air
Magical uses:	Fertility, gain, love
Recipe:	2½, 0, ⅛, 2 QB
Scent:	Sweet, woody, "cherry pipe tobacco"

Chickweed
Stellaria Media

Common names:	Adder's Mouth, Passerina, Starwort
Part used:	Leaves
Planet:	Moon
Element:	Water
Magical uses:	Animals, beauty, to stop gossip
Recipe:	2½, ¼, ⅛, 1¼ QB
Scent:	Bitter, sour, green

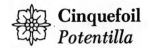

Cinnamon
Cinnamonum Zeylanicum

Common name:	Sweet Wood
Part used:	Bark, essence
Planet:	Mercury
Element:	Air
Magical uses:	Aphrodisiac, clairvoyance, consecration, divination, good luck, harmony, to increase the power of spells, inspiration, knowledge, love, material objects, meditation, money, passion, peace, prosperity, protection, psychic development & growth, tranquility, wealth, wisdom
Recipe:	2¹/₂, /₂, ¹/₈, 2¹/₄ QB
Scent:	Warm, sweet, spicy, mild

Both powdered cinnamon and its essence can cause irritation to the gastro-intestinal tract if taken internally.

Cinquefoil
Potentilla

Common names:	Five-finger Grass, Pentaphyllon, Sunkfield, Synkefoyle
Part used:	Leaves
Planet:	Mercury
Element:	Earth
Magical uses:	Clairvoyance, divination, exorcism, to increase the power of spells, inspiration, knowledge, love, magic, material objects, money, prosperity, protection, psychic protection, spell-breaking, wealth, wisdom
Recipe:	2¹/₂, ¹/₄, ¹/₈, 1¹/₂ QB
Scent:	Bittersweet, herby, green

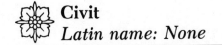

Civit
Latin name: None

Part used:	Essence (use artificial)
Planet:	Venus
Element:	Earth
Magical uses:	Animals, aphrodisiac, commanding, to increase the power of spells, love, passion, sensuality, virility
Scent:	Sweet, flowery, earthy, sensuous

Genuine civit comes from the musk gland of the civit cat. If you need to use civit in your incense, please use the artificially produced essence. It is almost as powerful, much less expensive, and a rare and beautiful animal doesn't have to be killed in the process.

Clary Sage
Salvia Sclarea

Common names:	Clear Eye, Muscatel Sage, Orvale
Part used:	Leaves and stems
Planet:	Mercury
Element:	Earth
Magical uses:	Clairvoyance, consecration, divination, harmony, inspiration, keep secrets, knowledge, love, material objects, meditation, peace, prosperity, protection, psychic development & growth, retention, tranquility, wealth, wisdom
Recipe:	$2^{1}/_{2}$, $^{1}/_{4}$, $^{1}/_{8}$, $1^{1}/_{2}$ Water
Scent:	Mild, bittersweet, herby

✤ Clover
Trifolium Repens

Common name:	White Clover
Part used:	Flowers
Planet:	Venus
Element:	Earth
Magical uses:	Animals, good luck, magic, money, to overcome opposition, protection, psychic protection, to stop gossip, strength
Recipe:	2¹/₂, ¹/₄, ¹/₈, 1 QB
Scent:	Dry, tart, grassy

✤ Cloves
Eugenia Aromatica

Common name:	Molucca Spice
Part used:	Buds, essence
Planet:	Sun
Element:	Fire
Magical uses:	Aphrodisiac, clairvoyance, divination, exorcism, to keep away negative forces, love, memory, peace of mind, protection, psychic development & growth, psychic protection, spell-breaking, to stop gossip
Recipe:	2, ¹/₄, ¹/₈, 1¹/₂ QB
Scent:	Warm, dry, sweet, spicy

Oil of cloves can cause minor skin irritation to people with sensitive skin.

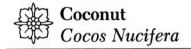 **Coconut**
Cocos Nucifera

Common name:	None
Part used:	Essence
Planet:	Moon
Element:	Water
Magical uses:	Beauty, fertility, gain
Scent:	Sweet, nutty, rich, tasty

 **Coltsfoot**
Tussilago Farara

Common names:	British Tobacco, Butterbur, Coughwort, Donnhove, Fieldhove, Horse Hoof
Part used:	Leaves
Planet:	Venus
Element:	Earth
Magical uses:	Working with animals, especially those with hooves
Recipe:	$2^{1}/_{2}$, $^{1}/_{2}$, $^{1}/_{8}$, $1^{1}/_{2}$ FW
Scent:	Bitter, green, strong

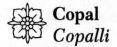

Comfrey
Symphtum Officinale

Common names:	Boneset, Bruisewort, Consolida, Gum Plant, Knitbone, Salsify, Slippery Root, Yallac
Part used:	Root
Planet:	Saturn
Element:	Earth
Magical uses:	Endings, exorcism, money, protection, release, safe journeys, spell-breaking
Recipe:	Loose only
Scent:	Bittersweet

Copal
Copalli

Common name:	Mexican Frankincense
Part used:	Gum
Planet:	Jupiter
Element:	Fire
Magical uses:	Consecration, contact other planes, exorcism, to increase the power of spells, meditation, protection, spell-breaking
Recipe:	1/2, 2, 1/8, 2 QB
Scent:	Etheral, clean, hint of frankincense

Coriander
Coriandrum Sativum

Common names:	Chinese Parsley, Culantro
Part used:	Seeds, essence
Planet:	Mars
Element:	Fire
Magical uses:	Aphrodisiac, clairvoyance, divination, fertility, gain, to keep secrets, love, retention
Recipe:	2, 1/2, 1/8, 1 1/4 QB
Scent:	Bittersweet, nutty

Crabgrass
Digitaria Sanguinalis

Common name:	Finger Grass, Wire Grass
Part used:	Leaves, stems, roots
Planet:	Mercury
Element:	Earth
Magical uses:	Determination, to keep secrets, material objects, overcome opposition, prosperity, retention, wealth
Recipe:	2 1/2, 1/4, 1/8, 2 Water
Scent:	Bittersweet, grassy, hay-like

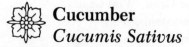

Cranesbill
Geranium Maculatum

Common names:	Alum Root, Chocolate Flower, Crowfoot, Storkbill, Tormentil, Wild Geranium
Part used:	Root
Planet:	Mars
Element:	Fire
Magical uses:	Animals, aphrodisiac, confidence, consecration, courage, exorcism, love, passion, protection, psychic protection, sensuality, spell-breaking, to stop gossip
Recipe:	2, 1/2, 1/4, 2 1/4 FW
Scent:	Bittersweet, tart, unusual

Cucumber
Cucumis Sativus

Common name:	None
Part used:	Seeds, essence
Planet:	Moon
Element:	Water
Magical uses:	Aphrodisiac, fertility, gain, love, psychic development & growth
Recipe:	1 1/4, 1 1/2, 1/8, 1 1/4 LF
Scent:	Damp, tart, bitter, subdued

✿ Damiana
Turnera Aphrodisiaca

Common name:	Mexican Damiana, Venus' Tonic
Part used:	Leaves
Planet:	Venus
Element:	Earth
Magical uses:	Aphrodisiac, contact other planes, to increase the power of spells, love, psychic development & growth, sensuality
Recipe:	2^1/$_2$, ^{1}/$_4$, ^{1}/$_8$, 1^1/$_2$ Water
Scent:	Bittersweet, herby, exotic

✿ Dandelion
Taraxacum Officinale

Common names:	Cankerwort, Irish Daisy, Lion's Tooth, Priest's Crown, Swine's Snout, Wild Endive
Part used:	Root
Planet:	Sun
Element:	Fire
Magical uses:	Animals, good luck, magic, psychic development & growth
Recipe:	Loose only
Scent:	Bittersweet, dry

Deer's Tongue
Liatus Odoratissima

Common names:	Hart's Tongue, Vanilla Leaf, Wild Vanilla
Part used:	Leaves, essence
Planet:	Venus
Element:	Earth
Magical uses:	Animals, love, to stop gossip
Recipe:	2, ¹/₂, ¹/₈, 1³/₄ FW
Scent:	Sweet, heady, vanilla-like

Dill
Anethum Graveolens

Common names:	Anethum, Meeting House Seed
Part used:	Seed, essence
Planet:	Mercury
Element:	Earth
Magical uses:	Determination, dreams, fertility, gain, harmony, to keep secrets, love, peace, protection, psychic protection, retention, rest, sleep, tranquility
Recipe:	2, ¹/₂, ¹/₈, 1¹/₄ LF
Scent:	Nutty, fruity, bittersweet

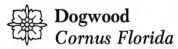 Dittany
Origanum Dictamnus

Common name:	Dittany of Crete, Greek Mint
Part used:	Leaves and stems, essence
Planet:	Venus
Element:	Earth
Magical uses:	To brighten disposition, clairvoyance, contact other planes, divination, happiness, materialization, meditation, psychic development & growth, visions
Recipe:	$2^{1}/_{2}$, $^{1}/_{4}$, $^{1}/_{8}$, $1^{1}/_{2}$ Water
Scent:	Herby, sweet, dreamy, mysterious

Dogwood
Cornus Florida

Common names:	Boxwood, Cornel, Green Ozier
Part used:	Bark
Planet:	Venus
Element:	Air
Magical uses:	Animals, fidelity, honesty, to keep secrets, prevent theft, protection, retention
Recipe:	$2^{1}/_{2}$, 0, $^{1}/_{8}$, $2^{1}/_{4}$ QB
Scent:	Subtle, sweet, woody

Dogwood is very toxic if taken internally, so be sure to keep it stored well out of reach of children and pets.

❋ Dragon's Blood
Daemonorops Draco/Calamus Draco

Common name:	Blume, Socotrine, Zanzibar Drop
Parts used:	Leaves, stems, resin
Planet:	Mars
Element:	Fire
Magical uses:	Animals, consecration, fidelity, good luck, honesty, to increase power of spells, love, magic, money, protection, psychic protection, strength, unexpected happenings , virility
Recipe:	1½, 1½, ⅛, 1¾ FW
Scent:	Etheral, mysterious, similar to frankincense

Many unscrupulous dealers will sell you "Poor Man's Dragon's Blood." It looks and smells much like the real thing, only it's made of talc, red sandalwood, and frankincense.

❋ Elder
Sambucus Canadensis

Common names:	Bat Tree, Devil's Eye, Elderberry, Ellhorn, Hollunder, Pipe Tree, Sureau, Tree of Doom
Part used:	Flowers
Planet:	Venus
Element:	Air
Magical uses:	Clairvoyance, commanding, compassion, consecration, contact other planes, divination, love, magic, messages from the dead, protection, psychic protection, transformation
Recipe:	Loose only
Scent:	Bittersweet, tart, burning leaves

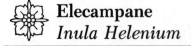 **Elecampane**
Inula Helenium

Common names:	Elf Dock, Elfwort, Horse Heal, Marchalan, Scabwort, Velvet Dock, Wild Sunflower
Part used:	Root
Planet:	Mercury
Element:	Earth
Magical uses:	Animals, attraction, beauty, love, magic
Recipe:	Loose only
Scent:	Bittersweet, tart, unusual

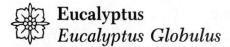 **Eucalyptus**
Eucalyptus Globulus

Common names:	Blue Gum, Dinkum, Stringy Bark Tree
Part used:	Leaves, essence
Planet:	Saturn
Element:	Earth
Magical uses:	Consecration, protection renewal
Recipe:	2, 1/2, 1/8, 1 3/4 FW
Scent:	Woody, leafy, green

Care should be taken when using eucalyptus oil; although it is used in many cold remedies, it is very toxic. If taken internally, an overdose can cause coma or even death.

Fennel
Foeniculum Vulgare

Common name:	Fenkel
Part used:	Seed, essence
Planet:	Mercury
Element:	Air
Magical uses:	Commanding, confidence, courage, fertility, gain, longevity, love, protection, psychic protection, strength
Recipe:	2, 1/2, 1/8, 1 1/2 Water
Scent:	Bittersweet, spicy, hint of licorice

Frankincense
Boswellia Carteri/Boswellia Thurifera

Common names:	Gum Thus, Luban, Olibanum
Part used:	Gum, essence
Planet:	Sun
Element:	Fire
Magical uses:	Clairvoyance, consecration, contact other planes, divination, exorcism, good luck, to increase power of spells, inspiration, knowledge, magic, meditation, protection, psychic development & growth, psychic protection, spell-breaking, success, transformation, wisdom
Recipe:	1/2, 2 1/2, 1/8, 1 1/2 FW
Scent:	Strong, heady, metallic, pure

🏵 Galangel
Alpinia Galanga

Common names:	African Ju Ju Powder, Catarrh Root, Chewing John, China Root, Laos, Low John
Part used:	Root, essence
Planet:	Mars
Element:	Fire
Magical uses:	Commanding, consecration, contact other planes, divine intervention, exorcism, good luck, to increase power of spells, law, love, magic, money, psychic protection, spell-breaking
Recipe:	2½, ¼, ⅛, 2¼ Water
Scent:	Semi-sweet, spicy, woody, fiery

🏵 Garlic
Allium Sativum

Common names:	Poor Man's Treacle, Suan
Part used:	Skin of Bulb
Planet:	Mars
Element:	Fire
Magical uses:	Aphrodisiac, clairvoyance, commanding, confidence, consecration, courage, divination, exorcism, longevity, magic, money, to overcome opposition, protection, spell-breaking, to stop gossip, strength, success
Recipe:	2, ½, ⅛, 1¼ Water
Scent:	Oniony, intense, martial

Ginger
Zingiber Officinale

Common name:	Ch'iang
Part used:	Root, essence
Planet:	Mars
Element:	Fire
Magical uses:	Aphrodisiac, love, passion, psychic development & growth, psychic protection, sensuality
Recipe:	Loose only
Scent:	Subtle, warm, spicy, peppery

Ginseng
Panax Quinquefolius/Panax Schin-seng

Common names:	Man-root, Red Berry, Tartar Root
Part used:	Root
Planet:	Saturn
Element:	Earth
Magical uses:	Aphrodisiac, gain, longevity, love, money, renewal, strength
Recipe:	$1/2$, 2, $1/8$, $1 3/4$ Water
Scent:	Powerful, penetrating, tart, bitter

Gotu Kola
Hydrocotyle Asiatica Minor

Common name:	Poor Man's Ginseng
Part used:	Leaves and stems
Planet:	Saturn
Element:	Earth
Magical uses:	Aphrodisiac, gain, longevity, psychic development & growth, renewal
Recipe:	2, 1/2, 1/8, 1 1/4 FW
Scent:	Bitter, tart, subtle

Grains of Paradise
Elettaria Cardamomum

Common names:	Cardamon, Egyptian Paradise Seed, Guinea Pepper, Love Pods
Part used:	Seeds, essence
Planet:	Venus
Element:	Earth
Magical uses:	Aphrodisiac, brightens disposition, fertility, gain, good luck, happiness, love, success
Recipe:	Loose only
Scent:	Semi-sweet, mild, unusual

Ground Ivy
Nepeta Hederacea

Common names:	Cat's Paw, Gillrun, Gort, Hedgemaids, Ivy, Turnhoof
Part used:	Leaves
Planet:	Saturn
Element:	Earth
Magical uses:	Animals, clairvoyance, divination, fidelity, honesty, to keep secrets, prevent theft, protection, renewal, retention, weddings
Recipe:	$2^1/_2$, $^1/_4$, $^1/_8$, 2 Water
Scent:	Subtle, bittersweet, herby, green

Hemlock
Tsuga Canadensis

Common names:	Canada Pitch Tree, Weeping Hemlock
Part used:	Needles, essence
Planet:	Saturn
Element:	Earth
Magical uses:	Fertility, protection, psychic protection, renewal, strength
Recipe:	$2^1/_2$, $^1/_4$, $^1/_8$, $1^1/_2$ QB
Scent:	Warm, gentle, pine-like

Do not confuse this hemlock with that of the poisonous plant of the same name. The hemlock used here, and throughout this book, is the evergreen tree called Hemlock.

Henna
Lawsonia Inermis

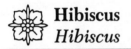

Common names:	Alcanna, Egyptian Privet, Medudi, Mignonette, Reseda
Part used:	Leaves
Planet:	Venus
Element:	Air
Magical uses:	Beauty, gain, gentleness, renewal
Recipe:	$2^1/_2$, $^1/_2$, $^1/_8$, $1^1/_2$ FW
Scent:	Gentle, robust, musky

Hibiscus
Hibiscus

Common name:	Rose Mallow
Part used:	Flowers, essence
Planet:	Moon
Element:	Water
Magical uses:	Clairvoyance, contact other planes, determination, divination, harmony, peace, psychic development & growth, tranquility
Recipe:	Loose only
Scent:	Bitter, tart

The smell of hibiscus flowers is very disappointing. To get the sweet smell of fresh hibiscus, you must use essence.

 **Holly**
Ilex

Common names:	Christ's Thorn, Holy Tree, Hulm, Tinne
Part used:	Leaves
Planet:	Mars
Element:	Fire
Magical uses:	Clairvoyance, consecration, divination, magic, protection, renewal, transformation, virility
Recipe:	2¹/₂, ¹/₄, ¹/₈, 1¹/₂ Water
Scent:	Green, leafy, woody

 Honeysuckle
Lonicera Fragrantissima

Common names:	Eglantine, Goat's Leaf, Woodbine
Part used:	Flowers, essence
Planet:	Mars
Element:	Fire
Magical uses:	Animals, clairvoyance, determination, divination, fidelity, good luck, honesty, inspiration, to keep secrets, knowledge, love, material objects, memory, money, peace of mind, to prevent theft, prosperity, psychic development & growth, retention, strength, weddings, wealth, wisdom
Recipe:	1¹/₂, 1, ¹/₈, 1¹/₂ QB
Scent:	Strong, tart, bittersweet

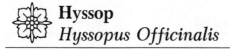

Horehound
Marrubium Vulgare

Common names:	Bull's Blood, Marrob, Marrubium, Seed of Horus
Part used:	Leaves and stems
Planet:	Saturn
Element:	Earth
Magical uses:	Animals, fidelity, honesty, to keep secrets, to prevent theft, protection, retention
Recipe:	2$^1/_2$, $^1/_4$, $^1/_8$, 1$^1/_4$ Water
Scent:	Bitter, strong, medicinal

Hyssop
Hyssopus Officinalis

Common name:	Holy Herb
Part used:	Leaves and stems, essence
Planet:	Jupiter
Element:	Fire
Magical uses:	Consecration, contact other planes, material objects, money, prosperity, protection, psychic development & growth, psychic protection, wealth
Recipe:	2$^1/_2$, $^1/_4$, $^1/_8$, 1$^3/_4$ Water
Scent:	Subtle, bitter

❈ Irish Moss
Chondrus Crispus

Common names:	Carrageen, Chondrus, Sea Moss, Sea Spirit
Part used:	"Leaves"
Planet:	Moon
Element:	Water
Magical uses:	Good luck, money, protection, rain, water rites
Recipe:	1/2, 2, 1/8, 2 1/2 FW
Scent:	Strong, musty, marsh mud

❈ Jalap
Ipomoea Jalapa

Common name:	High John the Conqueor
Part used:	Root, essence
Planet:	Saturn
Planet:	Earth
Magical uses:	Commanding, consecration, gambling, good luck, law, love, material objects, money, overcome opposition, prosperity, protection, success, wealth
Recipe:	1, 1 1/2, 1/8, 2 FW
Scent:	Bittersweet, heavy, syrupy

Morning glory root has been used for so long as an adulterant to jalap, that it is usually mistakenly called "High John." Of the two, jalap is both the original and the better herb.

✿ Jasmine
Jasminum Officinale

Common names:	Chameli, Sambac, Tore
Part used:	Flowers, essence
Planet:	Moon
Element:	Water
Magical uses:	Aphrodisiac, to brighten disposition, dreams, fertility, happiness, love, material objects, meditation, passion, prosperity, rest, sensuality, sleep, wealth, weddings
Recipe:	2, 1, $^1/_8$, $1^3/_4$ FW
Scent:	Mild, semisweet, herby

If you desire the rich sensuous smell of jasmine, you must use essence. When using it, care should be taken as it can cause allergic reactions in some people. Both the flowers and nectar of jasmine are very toxic. If taken internally, they can cause severe illness or even death; so handle and store them carefully.

✿ Juniper
Juniperus Communis

Common names:	Genevrier, Oil of Cade, Kuei
Part used:	Berries, essence
Planet:	Jupiter
Element:	Fire
Magical uses:	Animals, aphrodisiac, fertility, gain, to keep secrets, love, protection, to prevent theft, retention, strength
Recipe:	Loose only
Scent:	Woody, pine-like, rich, resin

Karaya
Sterculia

Common name:	Sterculia
Part used:	Gum
Planet:	Moon
Element:	Water
Magical uses:	Fertility, gain
Recipe:	None
Scent:	Mild, bread-like

Karaya gum is used almost exclusively by the incense making industry as a bonding agent; because it is the least expensive of any gum. It is usually sold in 100 lb. lots, so it is not commonly used by amateur incense makers. If you do manage to obtain some, handle it carefully. It can cause asthma attacks, hay fever, dermatitis, and even gastrointestinal disorders in some people.

Lady's Mantle
Alchemilla Vulgaris

Common names:	Lion's Foot, Nine Hooks, Stelleria
Part used:	Leaves
Planet:	Venus
Element:	Earth
Magical uses:	Animals, beauty, compassion, gentleness, modesty, weddings
Recipe:	2¹/₂, ¹/₄, ¹/₈, 1¹/₂ Water
Scent:	Mild, semisweet, grassy

Lavender
Lavendula Officinalis/Lavendula Vera

Common names:	Asarum, Elf Leaf, Khezama, Nard, Nardus
Part used:	Flowers, essence
Planet:	Mercury
Element:	Air
Magical uses:	Aphrodisiac, clairvoyance, consecration, divination, gentleness, good luck, harmony, to keep secrets, love, magic, memory, money, peace, peace of mind, protection, psychic development & growth, retention, tranquility, virility
Recipe:	2^1/$_2$, ^{1}/$_4$, ^{1}/$_8$, 1^1/$_2$ Water
Scent:	Bittersweet, flowery, different

Although lavender oil is widely used in perfumes and sprays; it can cause minor skin irritation or allergic reactions when exposed to direct sunlight.

Lemon
Citrus Limon

Common name:	None
Part used:	Essence
Planet:	Sun
Element:	Fire
Magical uses:	Beauty, contact other planes, to increase power of spells, strength,
Scent:	Sweet, zesty, tart

Though it is widely used, lemon oil has been known to cause allergic reactions in some people. It is also a suspected co-cancer causing agent.

Lemon Balm
Melissa Officinalis

Common names:	Balm, Bee Balm, Garden Balm, Honey Plant, Melissa, Sweet Balm
Part used:	Leaves, essence
Planet:	Jupiter
Element:	Fire
Magical uses:	To brighten disposition, compassion, endings, gentleness, happiness, longevity, love, psychic development & growth, release
Recipe:	$2^{1}/_{2}$, $^{1}/_{4}$, $^{1}/_{8}$, $1^{3}/_{4}$ QB
Scent:	Tart, bitter, green, intense

Lemon Grass
Cymbopogon Citratus

Common name:	Sereh
Part used:	"Leaves," essence
Planet:	Sun
Element:	Fire
Magical uses:	Clairvoyance, contact other planes, divination, fidelity, honesty, psychic development & growth, strength
Recipe:	$2^{1}/_{2}$, $^{1}/_{4}$, $^{1}/_{8}$, $2^{1}/_{4}$ Water
Scent:	Dry, grassy, tingles

Both the herb and essence of lemon grass are very toxic if taken internally, so be sure to store it well out of reach of children.

Lemon Verbena
Aloysia Triphylla

Common names:	Cedron, Herb Louisa, Verbena
Part used:	Leaves, essence
Planet:	Venus
Element:	Air
Magical uses:	To brighten disposition, dreams, exorcism, happiness, harmony, to increase power of spells, love, magic, peace, to prevent nightmares, protection, psychic protection, rest, sleep, spell-breaking, success, tranquility
Recipe:	$2^{1}/_{2}$, $^{1}/_{4}$, $^{1}/_{8}$, $1^{1}/_{2}$ QB
Scent:	Grassy, tart, hint of citrus

Life Everlasting
Gnaphalium Polycephalum

Common names:	Cat's Foot, Chafeweed, Cudweed, Sweet Balsam, White Balsam
Part used:	Flowers
Planet:	Venus
Element:	Air
Magical uses:	Animals, to keep secrets, longevity, memory, peace of mind, retention
Recipe:	$2^{1}/_{2}$, $^{1}/_{4}$, $^{1}/_{8}$, $1^{3}/_{4}$ Water
Scent:	Sour, bittersweet, wet fur

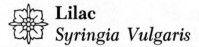

Lilac
Syringia Vulgaris

Common names:	Nila, Syringia
Part used:	Essence
Planet:	Jupiter
Element:	Fire
Magical uses:	Clairvoyance, divination, gentleness, harmony, love, memory, modesty, peace, peace of mind, psychic development & growth, psychic protection, recall past lives, tranquility
Scent:	Gentle, sweet, flowery, magical

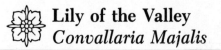

Lily of the Valley
Convallaria Majalis

Common names:	Convallaria, Jacob's Ladder, Male Lily, May Lily, May Bells, Our Lady's Tears
Part used:	Leaves, essence
Planet:	Venus
Element:	Air
Magical uses:	To brighten disposition, gentleness, happiness, modesty, protection
Recipe:	2¹/₂, ¹/₄, ¹/₈, 1³/₄ Water
Scent:	Bittersweet, herby, green

To get the rich, robust, and unusual fragrance of lily of the valley, you must use its essence. When using essence, care should be taken, as it can cause irregular heartbeat, digestive upset, and mental confusion if taken internally.

Linden
Tilla Europaea

Common names:	Basswood, Lime Tree, Spoonwood, Tilla, Wycopy
Part used:	Leaves, flowers, essence
Planet:	Jupiter
Element:	Fire
Magical uses:	Beauty, contact other planes, dreams, good luck, love, rest, sleep, weddings
Recipe:	$2^1/_4$, $^1/_4$, $^1/_8$, $1^3/_4$ Water
Scent:	Tangy, tart, grassy

Whenever you see a recipe that calls for lime or lime flowers, particularly in the older grimoirs, it actually means linden. The modern lime is a rather recent discovery, and is called a lime because it smells similar to linden.

Locust
Gleditsia Triacanthos

Common names:	American Acacia, False Acacia, Honey Locust
Part used:	Flowers
Planet:	Sun
Element:	Fire
Magical uses:	Contact other planes, gain, harmony, to increase power of spells, keep agreements & facts, meditation, money, peace, protection, psychic development & growth, tranquility
Recipe:	2, $^1/_2$, $^1/_8$, $1^1/_4$ QB
Scent:	Bittersweet, grassy, tart

The locust is the same family as the acacia and is sometimes used as an adulterant or replacement for it. They are both similar in scent, and as such, are difficult to tell apart.

Lovage
Levisticum Officinale

Common names:	Lavose, Sea Parsley
Part used:	Root
Planet:	Venus
Element:	Earth
Magical uses:	Aphrodisiac, consecration, love, money, protection, psychic protection
Recipe:	2½, ¼, ⅛, 1¾ QB
Scent:	Rich, sweet, fresh celery seeds

Mace
Myristica Officinalis/ Myristica Fragrans

Common name:	Macis, Banda Fruit
Part used:	Fruit
Planet:	Mercury
Element:	Air
Magical uses:	Fertility, gain, good luck, love, protection
Recipe:	1½, 1, ⅛, 1¼ QB
Scent:	Nutty, burny, similar to nutmeg

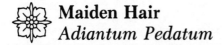

Maiden Hair
Adiantum Pedatum

Common names:	Five-finger Fern, Rock Fern, Venus's Hair
Part used:	Leaves and stems
Planet:	Venus
Element:	Earth
Magical uses:	Aphrodisiac, beauty, gentleness, harmony, love, modesty, peace, tranquility
Recipe:	$2^1/_2$, $^1/_4$ $^1/_8$, $1^3/_4$ Water
Scent:	Light, mild, grassy

Mandrake
Podophyllum Peltatum/ Mandragora Officinarum

Common names:	Alraun, Baaras, Duck's Foot, Ground Lemon, Herb of Circe, Mandragora, May Apple, Satan's Apple, Wild Jalap
Part used:	Root
Planet:	Mercury
Element:	Earth
Magical uses:	Animals, aphrodisiac, fertility, love, magic, material objects, money, prosperity, protection, psychic development & growth, sensuality, virility, wealth
Recipe:	2, $^1/_2$, $^1/_8$, 2 FW
Scent:	Mild, woody, subtle yet penetrating

Mandrake root is sometimes adulterated or even replaced with bryony root. Some unscrupulous dealers will even use a blend of orris root, solomons seal, and sandalwood and pass it off as powdered mandrake.

Marigold
Calendula Officinalis

Common names:	Calendula, Golds, Ruddes, Summer's Bride, Verrucaria
Part used:	Flowers
Planet:	Sun
Element:	Fire
Magical uses:	To brighten disposition, clairvoyance, commanding, divination, dreams, good luck, happiness, love, material objects, memory, money, peace of mind, prosperity, protection, psychic development & growth, renewal, rest, sleep, success, wealth
Recipe:	$2^{1}/_{2}$, $^{1}/_{2}$, $^{1}/_{8}$, $1^{1}/_{4}$ FW
Scent:	Grassy, strong, bitter

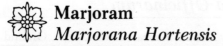

Marjoram
Marjorana Hortensis

Common names:	Amaracus, Khezama, Mountain Mint, Wintersweet
Part used:	Leaves, essence
Planet:	Venus
Element:	Air
Magical uses:	Animals, to brighten disposition, happiness, harmony, love, peace, protection, psychic development & growth, psychic protection, tranquility, weddings
Recipe:	Loose only
Scent:	Bittersweet, herby

Marjoram oil can cause minor allergic reactions and/or skin irritation.

Meadowsweet
Filipendula Ulmaria

Common names:	Bridewort, Dolloff, Gravel Root, Meadow Queen, Meadwort, Queen of the Meadow, Trumpet Weed
Part used:	Leaves and stems
Planet:	Jupiter
Element:	Fire
Magical uses:	Domestic tranquility, gentleness, good luck, harmony, love, money, peace, tranquility, weddings
Recipe:	2¹/₂, ¹/₂, ¹/₈, 1³/₄ FW
Scent:	Unusual, herby, rubbery, green

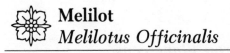 # Melilot
Melilotus Officinalis

Common names:	Hart's Tree, Hay Flowers, King's Clover, Sweet Clover, Sweet Lucerne
Part used:	Leaves
Planet:	Venus
Element:	Earth
Magical uses:	Animals, to brighten disposition, commanding, endings, good luck, happiness, overcome opposition, psychic protection, release, strength
Recipe:	2¹/₂, ¹/₄, ¹/₈, 1³/₄ Water
Scent:	Mild, grassy, haylike, hint of herbs

Menthol
Mentha Javanica

Common name:	Chinese Peppermint Oil
Part used:	Crystals, essence
Planet:	Mars
Element:	Fire
Magical Uses:	Anti-aphrodisiac, break off an affair, commanding, endings, exorcism, to increase power of spells, psychic development & growth, release spell-breaking
Recipe:	1/4, 2 1/2, 1/8, 1 3/4 Water
Scent:	Strong, cold, minty, penetrating

Because of the high cost of distilling, most menthol is now artificially produced.

Mistletoe
Phoradendron Flavescens/ Viscum⎮Album

Common names:	All-heal, Birdlime, Golden Bough, Loranthus
Part used:	Leaves, berries
Planet:	Sun
Element:	Fire
Magical uses:	Animals, consecration, contact other planes, fertility, gain, good luck, love, magic, protection, psychic protection, renewal, success, virility
Recipe:	2, 1, 1/8, 1 1/2 FW
Scent:	Etheral, unique, woody, herby

If taken internally, Mistletoe berries can cause acute stomach and intestinal irritation, poisoning, or even death.

Motherwort
Leonorus Cardiaca

Common names:	Lion's Ear, Throw-wort
Part used:	Leaves
Planet:	Venus
Element:	Earth
Magical uses:	Animals, to brighten disposition, compassion, dreams, fertility, gentleness, happiness, harmony, love, peace, rest, sleep, tranquility
Recipe:	2½, ¼, ⅛, 2 Water
Scent:	Strong, grassy, bitter

Mugwort
Artemisia Vulgaris

Common names:	Artemisia, Felon Herb, Moxa, Sailor's Tobacco, St. John's Plant, Witch Herb
Part used:	Leaves
Planet:	Venus
Element:	Air
Magical uses:	Aphrodisiac, clairvoyance, consecration, divination, dreams, longevity, magic, to prevent theft, protection, psychic development & growth, psychic protection, rest, sleep, strength
Recipe:	2½, ¼, ⅛, 1½ Water
Scent:	Bitter, tart, hint of sage

Musk
Latin name: None

Common name:	Green Powder
Part used:	Essence, use artificial
Planet:	Venus
Element:	Earth
Magical uses:	Animals, aphrodisiac, commanding, confidence, consecration, courage, good luck, to increase power of spells, love, passion, sensuality, strength, success, virility
Scent:	Full-bodied, earthy, sweet, sensuous

Genuine musk comes from the musk glands of the Musk Deer. I strongly urge you to use only artificially produced musk oil. It is far less expensive, easy to obtain, smells almost the same as real musk, and a beautiful animal doesn't have to give up its life to produce it.

Musk Root
Ferula Sumbul

Common names:	Ferula, Jatamansi, Sumbul Root
Part used:	Root
Planet:	Venus
Element:	Earth
Magical uses:	Same as musk
Recipe:	2$\frac{1}{2}$, $\frac{1}{4}$, $\frac{1}{8}$, 1$\frac{3}{4}$ Water
Scent:	Lusty, earthy, warm, hint of musk

 **Mustard**
Brassica

Common name:	None
Part used:	Seed, essence
Planet:	Mars
Element:	Fire
Magical uses:	Aphrodisiac, commanding, exorcism, fertility, gain, love, passion, protection, sensuality, spell-breaking, strength, success, virility
Recipe:	$1/2$, 2, $1/8$, $1^1/2$ FW
Scent:	Warm, fiery, peppery

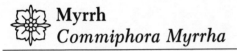 **Myrrh**
Commiphora Myrrha

Common names:	Antew, Bowl, Didin, Karam, Mor, Stacte, Mu-Yao
Part used:	Gum, essence
Planet:	Sun
Element:	Fire
Magical uses:	To brighten disposition, compassion, consecration, endings, exorcism, good luck, happiness, magic, material objects, prosperity, protection, psychic protection, release, spell-breaking, success, transformation, wealth
Recipe:	1, 2, $1/8$, $1^3/4$ QB
Scent:	unusual, rubbery, balloons

Myrtle
Myrica Cerifera/Myrtus Communis

Common names:	Bayberry, Candleberry, Hadassim, Tallow Shrub, Wax Berry, Wax Myrtle
Part used:	Leaves, essence
Planet:	Venus
Element:	Earth
Magical uses:	Aphrodisiac, to brighten disposition, compassion, fertility, happiness, longevity, love, magic, material objects, money, prosperity, wealth, weddings
Recipe:	2¹/₂, ¹/₄, ¹/₈, 1³/₄ QB
Scent:	Semisweet, herby, leafy

Nettle
Urtica Dioica

Common names:	Stinging Nettle, Wergulu
Part used:	Leaves
Planet:	Mars
Element:	Fire
Magical uses:	Aphrodisiac, exorcism, magic, protection, psychic protection, spell-breaking
Recipe:	1¹/₂, 1, ¹/₈, 1¹/₂ QB
Scent:	Bitter, biting, green, tart

For ages, nettle has been known for its stinging quality. Handle it carefully, as it can cause skin irritation.

Nutmeg
Myristica Fragrans

Common name:	Calabach, Plume
Part used:	Seed, essence
Planet:	Jupiter
Element:	Fire
Magical uses:	Aphrodisiac, clairvoyance, divination, dreams, fertility, gain, love, meditation, money, protection, psychic development & growth, rest, sleep
Recipe:	2, 1, $^1/_8$, $1^1/_2$ FW
Scent:	Bittersweet, nutty, hint of spice and licorice

If taken internally, nutmeg oil is toxic. It can cause flushed skin, irregular heartbeat, hallucinations, and death.

Oak
Quercus

Common name:	Tanner's Bark, Hu
Part used:	Leaves, bark
Planet:	Jupiter
Element:	Fire
Magical uses:	Commanding, confidence, courage, fertility, to keep secrets, longevity, magic, material objects, overcome opposition, prosperity, protection, retention, strength, success, virility, wealth
Recipe:	$2^1/_2$, $^1/_4$, $^1/_8$, $1^1/_2$ Water
Scent:	Burning autumn leaves

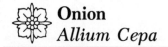

Oakmoss
Latin names: Many

Common name:	Oak Scale
Part used:	Plant
Planet:	Moon
Element:	Water
Magical uses:	Clairvoyance, contact other planes, divination, exorcism, magic, spell-breaking
Recipe:	2¼, ½, ⅛, 1½ QB
Scent:	Unusual, bittersweet, "other worldly"

Oak moss is not just one plant, but a combination of several types of moss and lichens. They range in color from white and gray to various shades of green. They can be found growing mostly on oak and other hardwood trees that are weak or diseased.

Onion
Allium Cepa

Common name:	Victory Root
Part used:	Skin of bulb
Planet:	Mars
Element:	Fire
Magical uses:	Aphrodisiac, clairvoyance, commanding, consecration, divination, exorcism, magic, overcome opposition, protection, spell-breaking, to stop gossip, success
Recipe:	2, 1, ⅛, 1¼ QB
Scent:	Strong, oniony, martial

Any type of onion skin may be used; however, I prefer to use white onion skins. They are much sweeter and milder than either the yellow or red onions.

Orange
Citrus Aurantium/Citrus Sinensis

Common name:	Kyul, Neroli
Part used:	Flowers, essence
Planet:	Sun
Element:	Fire
Magical uses:	Beauty, brighten disposition, fertility, good luck, happiness, love, material objects, money, prosperity, wealth, weddings
Recipe:	2^1/$_2$, ^{1}/$_2$, ^{1}/$_8$, 1^3/$_4$ FW
Scent:	Mild, bittersweet, similar to linden

Like most flowers, dried orange flowers have almost no scent. To get the tasty smell of oranges, you must use essence. Handle orange essence with care as it can cause allergic reactions such as swelling skin, blisters, headaches, dizziness, and shortness of breath.

Orchid
Orchidaceae

Common name:	None
Part used:	Essence
Planet:	Venus
Element:	Air
Magical uses:	Aphrodisiac, beauty, love
Scent:	Sweet, flowery, sensuous

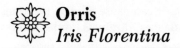

Oregano
Origanum Vulgare

Common names:	Origanum, Wild Marjoram
Part used:	Leaves
Planet:	Venus
Element:	Air
Magical uses:	Animals, to brighten disposition, happiness, harmony, love, peace, protection, psychic development & growth, tranquility, weddings
Recipe:	$2^{1/2}$, $^{1/4}$, $^{1/8}$, $1^{1/2}$ QB
Scent:	Sweet, herby, fresh

Orris
Iris Florentina

Common names:	Florentine Iris, Iris Root, Love Root, Queen Elizabeth Root
Part used:	Root, essence
Planet:	Venus
Element:	Earth
Magical uses:	Commanding, exorcism, love, protection, spell-breaking, to stop gossip
Recipe:	$1^{1/4}$, $1^{1/4}$, $^{1/8}$, 2 FW
Scent:	Semisweet, woody, dry, mild

The sale of pure orris root extract is banned in the U.S.A. because it causes severe allergic reactions, which include hay fever, asthma, stuffy nose, red and swollen eyes, and infantile eczema. Any orris extract that you can buy is either artificially produced or greatly watered down.

Parsley

Petroselinum Crispum/ Petroselinum Sativum

Common name:	Death Plant, Inn-Sai
Part used:	Leaves, essence
Planet:	Saturn
Element:	Earth
Magical uses:	Aphrodisiac, to brighten disposition, clairvoyance, contact other planes, divination, happiness, meditation, psychic development & growth
Recipe:	$1^{1}/_{2}$, 1, $^{1}/_{8}$, $1^{1}/_{2}$ FW
Scent:	Tart, green, bitter

Parsley oil can cause allergic reactions which include redness, rash, and swelling of the skin if it is exposed to direct sunlight.

Patchouli
Pogostemon Cablin/ Pogostemon Heyneanus

Common name:	Graveyard Dust, Puchaput
Part used:	Leaves, essence
Planet:	Venus
Element:	Earth
Magical uses:	Clairvoyance, commanding contact other planes, divination, exorcism, to increase power of spells, love, magic, memory, peace of mind, protection, psychic protection, sensuality, spell-breaking
Recipe:	$2^{1}/_{2}$, $^{1}/_{4}$, $^{1}/_{8}$, $1^{3}/_{4}$ Water
Scent:	Heavy, dry, dusty, earthy

Patchouli oil can cause minor allergic reactions in some people.

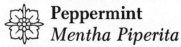 Pennyroyal
Hedeona Pulegioides/Mentha Puleg

Common names:	Mosquito Plant, Piliolerial, Pudding Grass, Squaw Mint, Tickweed
Part used:	Leaves, essence
Planet:	Venus
Element:	Air
Magical uses:	Endings, harmony, love, peace, protection, release, tranquility
Recipe:	2¹/₂, ¹/₄, ¹/₈, 1¹/₂ Water
Scent:	Sweet, herby, minty

Peppermint
Mentha Piperita

Common names:	Brandy Mint, Lamb's Mint, Lammint
Part used:	Essence
Planet:	Venus
Element:	Air
Magical uses:	Animals, aphrodisiac, to brighten disposition, consecration, dreams, endings, good luck, happiness, love, material objects, money, prosperity, protection, psychic development & growth, release, renewal, rest, sleep, transformation, wealth
Scent:	Cool, fresh, sweet, "minty"

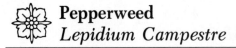

Pepperweed
Lepidium Campestre

Common name:	Pepper Grass
Part Used:	Leaves
Planet:	Mars
Element:	Fire
Magical uses:	Aphrodisiac, commanding, exorcism, passion, sensuality, spell-breaking
Recipe:	Loose only
Scent:	Bitter, strong, biting, peppery

If you feel that you must use pepper in your incense, then use pepperweed instead. Real pepper is much too powerful and harmful to your health to even consider.

Pine
Pinus

Common name:	Evergreen
Part used:	Needles, essence
Planet:	Saturn
Element:	Earth
Magical uses:	Animals, clairvoyance, compassion, consecration, divination, fertility, magic, protection, psychic protection, strength
Recipe:	$2^{1/2}$, 0, $^{1}/_{8}$, $1^{1}/_{4}$ QB
Scent:	Mild, fresh, evergreen

Pine oil can cause irritation of the skin and mucous membranes. If taken internally, it can cause nausea, vomiting, dizziness, and convulsions.

Plantain
Plantago Major

Common names:	Cuckoo's Bread, Ripple Grass, Snakeweed, Weybroed, Whiteman's Foot
Part used:	Leaves
Planet:	Jupiter
Element:	Fire
Magical uses:	Animals, determination, fertility, gain, honesty, love, protection, to stop gossip, transformation
Recipe:	$2^{1}/_{2}$, $^{1}/_{2}$, $^{1}/_{8}$, $1^{1}/_{2}$ FW
Scent:	Green, tart, grassy, bitter

Pomegranate
Punica Granatum

Common names:	Chinese Apple, Grenadier, Malicorio
Part used:	Peel
Planet:	Venus
Element:	Earth
Magical uses:	Fertility, gain, to keep secrets, material objects, prosperity, renewal, retention
Recipe:	$2^{1}/_{2}$, $^{1}/_{4}$, $^{1}/_{8}$, $2^{1}/_{4}$ Water
Scent:	Mild, woody, hint of spice

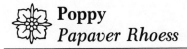

Poppy
Papaver Rhoess

Common name:	Corn Rose, Headache, Manseed
Part used:	Flowers
Planet:	Moon
Element:	Water
Magical uses:	Clairvoyance, commanding, compassion, consolation, divination, dreams, fertility, gain, harmony, love, material objects, peace, prosperity, rest, sleep, tranquility, wealth
Recipe:	Loose only
Scent:	Subtle, sleepy, many different levels

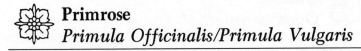

Primrose
Primula Officinalis/Primula Vulgaris

Common names:	Butter Rose, Drelip, English Cowslip, Fairy Cups, Herb Peter, Our Lady's Keys, Password
Part used:	Flowers, essence
Planet:	Venus
Element:	Air
Magical uses:	Animals, compassion, dreams, harmony, longevity, love, magic, peace, protection, renewal, rest, sleep, to stop gossip, tranquility
Recipe:	2$^{1}/_{2}$, $^{1}/_{4}$, $^{1}/_{8}$, 1$^{1}/_{2}$ Water
Scent:	Bittersweet, tart, herby

Psyllium
Plantago Psyllium

Common name:	Fleaseed
Part used:	Seed
Planet:	Jupiter
Element:	Fire
Magical uses:	Animals, determination, fertility, fidelity, gain, honesty, love, protection, to stop gossip, transformation
Recipe:	Loose only
Scent:	Sour, bitter, nutty

Quassia
Quassia Amara

Common names:	Bitter Ash, Bitterwood
Part used:	Wood
Planet:	Saturn
Element:	Earth
Magical uses:	Compassion, endings, love, protection, release
Recipe:	2^{1}/$_{2}$, 0, ^{1}/$_{8}$, 1^{3}/$_{4}$ Water
Scent:	Sweet, woody, similar to sandalwood

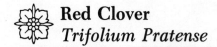

Red Clover
Trifolium Pratense

Common names:	Purple Clover, Trefoil, Wild Clover
Part used:	Flowers
Planet:	Venus
Element:	Earth
Magical uses:	Animals, good luck, magic, money, overcome opposition, protection, psychic protection, to stop gossip, strength
Recipe:	2^1/$_2$, ^{1}/$_4$, ^{1}/$_8$, 1^1/$_4$ Water
Scent:	Bittersweet, grassy, hay-like

Whenever you come across an incense recipe that calls for clover, it almost always means red clover. It is a little harder to obtain, but is much sweeter, milder and easier to burn than regular white clover.

Red Sandalwood
Pterocarpus Santalinus

Common names:	Red Sanders, Rubywood, Sappan
Part used:	Wood
Planet:	Venus
Element:	Earth
Magical uses:	Fidelity, honesty, love, protection
Recipe:	2^1/$_2$, 0, ^{1}/$_8$, 1^1/$_2$ Water
Scent:	Like Sandalwood, woody, sweet, clean

Reed
Phragmites Communis

Common names:	Cane, Carrizo, Feather Grass
Part used:	Leaves
Planet:	Moon
Element:	Water
Magical uses:	Animals, clairvoyance, divination, modesty, water rites, weather
Recipe:	$2^1/_2$, $^1/_4$, $^1/_4$, $1^3/_4$ Water
Scent:	Mild, green, moist

Rose
Rosa

Common name:	Love Flower
Part used:	Flowers, essence
Planet:	Venus
Element:	Air
Magical uses:	Aphrodisiac, beauty, clairvoyance, compassion, consecration, contact other planes, divination, good luck, harmony, to keep secrets, longevity, love, magic, memory, peace, peace of mind, retention, tranquility, transformation, weddings
Recipe:	$2^1/_2$, $^1/_4$, $^1/_8$, $1^1/_4$ QB
Scent:	Bittersweet, flowery, seductive

Pure rose essence is very expensive and almost impossible to obtain. It takes over 25,000 pounds of rose petals to produce just one liter of rose oil! Needless to say, whenever you buy rose oil it is either artificially produced or contains very little pure rose essence.

Rose Geranium
Pelargonium Graveolens

Common name:	None
Part used:	Leaves, essence
Planet:	Mars
Element:	Fire
Magical uses:	Animals, aphrodisiac, confidence, consecration, courage, exorcism, love, passion, protection, psychic protection, sensuality, spell-breaking, to stop gossip
Recipe:	2, 1/2, 1/8 1 1/4 FW
Scent:	Tart, bitter, sour

Rosemary
Rosmarius Officinalis

Common names:	Compass Weed, Guardrobe, Incensier, Polar Plant, Sea Dew
Part used:	Leaves, essence
Planet:	Sun
Element:	Fire
Magical uses:	Aphrodisiac, to brighten disposition, confidence, consecration, courage, endings, fidelity, good luck, happiness, honesty, inspiration, knowledge, longevity, love, meditation, memory, peace of mind, to prevent theft, protection, psychic development & growth, release, strength, transformation, water rites, weddings, wisdom
Recipe:	2 1/2, 1/4, 1/8 1 1/4 Water
Scent:	Sweet, herby, fresh

Rosemary oil can be toxic if taken internally.

Rue
Ruta Graveolens

Common names:	Herb of Grace, Herb of Repentence
Part used:	Leaves and stems, essence
Planet:	Saturn
Element:	Earth
Magical uses:	Compassion, consecration, good luck, karma, longevity, love, magic, protection, psychic development & growth, psychic protection,
Recipe:	2¹/₂, ¹/₄, ¹/₈, 1¹/₂ Water
Scent:	Bitter, somber, cigar-like

Safflower
Carthamus Tinctorius

Common names:	American Saffron, Begger's Crocus
Part used:	Flowers, essence
Planet:	Sun
Element:	Fire
Magical uses:	Clairvoyance, commanding, divination, exorcism, magic, psychic development & growth, spell-breaking
Recipe:	2¹/₂, ¹/₄, ¹/₈, 1¹/₄ Water
Scent:	Bittersweet, tart, herby

Safflower is used almost exclusively as a substitute for saffron. It doesn't smell quite as sweet or mild, but it is more economical to use. When storing safflower oil, be sure to keep it tightly sealed. Exposure to fresh air for any length of time causes it to get rancid.

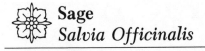

Sage
Salvia Officinalis

Common names:	Salvia, Sawge
Part used:	Leaves, essence
Planet:	Mercury
Element:	Earth
Magical uses:	Aphrodisiac, clairvoyance, consecration, divination, domestic harmony, inspiration, to keep secrets, knowledge, longevity, love, material objects, meditation, peace, prosperity, psychic development & growth, psychic protection, retention, tranquility, wealth, weddings, wisdom
Recipe:	2$\frac{1}{2}$, $\frac{1}{4}$, $\frac{1}{8}$, 1$\frac{1}{2}$ Water
Scent:	Sweet, herby, "Sunday chicken"

St. Johnswort
Hypericum Perforatum

Common names:	Amber, Goatweed, Hypericum, Klamathweed
Part Used:	Leaves
Planet:	Sun
Element:	Fire
Magical uses:	Animals, commanding confidence, courage, exorcism, good luck, to increase power of spells, magic, overcome opposition, protection, psychic protection, spell-breaking, strength, success
Recipe:	2$\frac{1}{2}$, $\frac{1}{4}$, $\frac{1}{8}$, 1$\frac{3}{4}$ Water
Scent:	Bittersweet, herby, heady

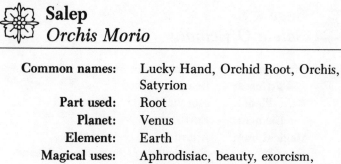

Salep
Orchis Morio

Common names:	Lucky Hand, Orchid Root, Orchis, Satyrion
Part used:	Root
Planet:	Venus
Element:	Earth
Magical uses:	Aphrodisiac, beauty, exorcism, gambling, good luck, magic, money, psychic protection, spell-breaking, success
Recipe:	Loose only
Scent:	Dry, woody, powdery

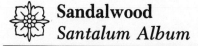

Sandalwood
Santalum Album

Common names:	Sanders, White Sandalwood, White Sanders, Yellow Sandalwood
Part used:	Powdered wood, essence
Planet:	Mercury
Element:	Air
Magical uses:	Clairvoyance, consecration, contact other planes, divination, good luck, meditation, protection, psychic development & growth, success
Recipe:	2½, 0, ⅛, 1¾ Water
Scent:	Woody, sweet, clean

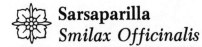 **Sarsaparilla**
Smilax Officinalis

Common names:	Bamboo Briar, Bramble Vine
Part used:	Root
Planet:	Mars
Element:	Fire
Magical uses:	Aphrodisiac, to keep secrets, protection, retention
Recipe:	2, 1/2, 1/8, 1 1/2 FW
Scent:	Discreet, mint of sweet wood

 **Sassafras**
Sassafras Albidum/Sassafras Officinalis

Common names:	Argue Tree, Cinnamon Wood, Saxifrax
Part used:	Bark of root, essence
Planet:	Saturn
Element:	Earth
Magical uses:	Compassion, gentleness
Recipe:	2 1/2, 1/4, 1/8, 2 Water
Scent:	Semisweet, woody, hint of "root beer"

Sassafras essence can cause dermatitus to those with sensitive skin.

Savory
Satureia Hortensis

Common names:	Bean Herb, Satyr's Herb
Part used:	Leaves
Planet:	Venus
Element:	Air
Magical uses:	Animals, aphrodisiac, to attract males, love, passion, sensuality, virility
Recipe:	$2^1/2$, $^1/2$, $^1/4$, 2 FW
Scent:	Semisweet, herby

Saw Palmetto
Serenoa Serulata/Serenoa Repens

Common names:	Dwarf Palmetto, Fan Palm, Pan Palm, Sabal
Part used:	Berries
Planet:	Venus
Element:	Earth
Magical uses:	Aphrodisiac, to attract males, fertility, gain, love, passion, sensuality
Recipe:	2, $^1/2$, $^1/8$, $1^1/4$ Water
Scent:	Strong, heavy, resin-like

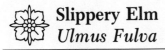

Scammony
Convolvukus Scammonia

Common names:	Syrian Bindweed, Wild Jalap
Part used:	Root
Planet:	Saturn
Element:	Earth
Magical uses:	Consecration, gambling, good luck, law, love, material objects, money, prosperity, protection, success, wealth
Recipe:	2 1/2, 1/4, 1/8, 2 Water
Scent:	Sweet, penetrating, candy-like

Slippery Elm
Ulmus Fulva

Common name:	Elm, Yu, Indian Elm
Part used:	Bark
Planet:	Saturn
Element:	Earth
Magical uses:	Commanding, endings, exorcism, gentleness, magic, protection, release, spell-breaking, to stop gossip
Recipe:	2, 1/2, 1/8, 1 1/2 FW
Scent:	Mild, woody, clean

Solomon's Seal
Polygonatum Multiflorum

Common names:	Dropberry, Lady's Seal, St. Mary's Seal, Sealwort
Part used:	Root, essence
Planet:	Saturn
Element:	Earth
Magical uses:	Consecration, exorcism, good luck, inspiration, knowledge, material objects, money, prosperity, protection, psychic development & growth, psychic protection, spell-breaking, success, wealth, wisdom
Recipe:	$2^{1}/_{2}$, $^{1}/_{4}$, $^{1}/_{8}$, $1^{3}/_{4}$ Water
Scent:	Strong, semisweet, celery-like

Southernwood
Artemisia Abronatum

Common names:	Appleringie, Garde-robe, Lad's Love, Maiden's Ruin, Old Man
Part used:	Leaves and stems
Planet:	Mercury
Element:	Earth
Magical uses:	Animals, aphrodisiac, clairvoyance, contact other planes, determination, divination, exorcism, love, magic, to overcome opposition, psychic development & growth, spell-breaking, transformation
Recipe:	$2^{1}/_{2}$, $^{1}/_{4}$, $^{1}/_{8}$, $1^{3}/_{4}$ Water
Scent:	Strong, earthy, peppery

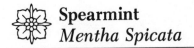

Spearmint
Mentha Spicata

Common names:	Green Mint, Green Spine, Lamb's Mint, Our Lady's Mint, Sage of Bethlehem
Part used:	Essence
Planet:	Venus
Element:	Air
Magical uses:	Animals, aphrodisiac, to brighten disposition, consecration, dreams, endings, good luck, happiness, love, material objects, money, prosperity, protection, psychic development & growth, release, renewal, rest, sleep, transformation, wealth
Scent:	Fresh, cool, "minty"

Spearmint essence can cause minor skin irritation or rash to those with sensitive skin.

Spikenard
Aralia Racemosa/ Nardostachys Jatamansi

Common names:	American Spikenard, Indian Root, Life of Man, Nard, Old Man's Root, Onycha, Pettymorell, Pigeon Weed, Spignet
Part used:	Root
Planet:	Saturn
Element:	Earth
Magical uses:	Animals, commanding, love, money, psychic protection
Recipe:	2$^1/_2$, $^1/_4$, $^1/_8$, 1$^3/_4$ Water
Scent:	Dry, woody, subtle

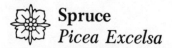 Spruce
Picea Excelsa

Common name:	Norway Pine
Part used:	Needles
Planet:	Saturn
Element:	Earth
Magical uses:	Fertility, protection, psychic protection, strength
Recipe:	2$^1/_2$, $^1/_2$, $^1/_8$, 1$^1/_2$ FW
Scent:	Mild, woody, piney

Star Anise
Illicium Anisatum/Illicium Verum

Common names:	Badiana, Chinese Anise
Part used:	Seeds, essence
Planet:	Mercury
Element:	Air
Magical uses:	Aphrodisiac, clairvoyance, consecration, contact other planes, divination, fertility, gain, good luck, love, money, prevent nightmares, protection, psychic development & growth, psychic protection
Recipe:	2$^1/_2$, $^1/_2$, $^1/_8$, 1$^1/_2$ QB
Scent:	Mild, bittersweet, hint of licorice

Whenever a recipe calls for anise, I always use star anise instead. It may be a little harder to obtain, but it is much sweeter and more fragrant than regular anise.

Storax
Liquidamber Orientalis

Common names:	Amber, Liquid Amber, Neteph, Stracte, Styrax
Part used:	Gum, essence
Planet:	Mercury
Element:	Earth
Magical uses:	Commanding, consecration, contact other planes, exorcism, to increase power of spells, magic, protection, psychic protection, spell-breaking, strength, success
Recipe:	$1/4$, 2, 0, 1 FW
Scent:	Heavy, sweet, resiny

I strongly suggest that if you wish to use storax, you try using its essence. Storax gum is very sticky and hard to handle; it can also cause minor skin irritation. If taken internally, it is mildly toxic, and can cause urinary problems.

Strawberry
Fragaria Vesca

Common name:	Wild Strawberry, Ttalgi
Part used:	Leaves, essence
Planet:	Venus
Element:	Earth
Magical uses:	Beauty, clairvoyance, divination, fertility, gain, love
Recipe:	$2^1/2$, $1/4$, $1/8$, $1^3/4$ QB
Scent:	Dry, bitter, green

Strawberry leaves have no juicy tasty strawberry scent. To get that sweet and full-bodied aroma, you must use essence.

Sunflower
Helianthus Annus

Common name:	Marigold of Peru
Part used:	Petals
Planet:	Sun
Element:	Fire
Magical uses:	Clairvoyance, commanding, divination, dreams, fertility, gain, good luck, love, material objects, money, prosperity, protection, psychic development & growth, rest, sleep, success, wealth
Recipe:	2¹/₂, ¹/₄, ¹/₈ 1¹/₄ Water
Scent:	Subtle, grassy, hint of tartness

Sweet Gum
Liquidamber Styraciflua

Common names:	American Liquid Amber, Copalm, Gum Tree, Opossum Tree
Part used:	Bark
Planet:	Mercury
Element:	Earth
Magical uses:	Exorcism, to increase power of spells, protection, spell-breaking, success
Recipe:	2¹/₂, 0, ¹/₈, 2¹/₄ Water
Scent:	Semisweet, woody, hint of storax

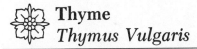

Tarragon
Artemisia Dracunculus

Common names:	Dragon Herb, Estragon, Little Dragon
Part used:	Leaves and stems
Planet:	Mars
Element:	Fire
Magical uses:	Animals, aphrodisiac, commanding, confidence, courage, to keep secrets, love, passion, to prevent theft, protection, retention, sensuality, strength, virility
Recipe:	Loose only
Scent:	Fiery, spicy, herby, bittersweet

Thyme
Thymus Vulgaris

Common name:	Bitter Mint
Part used:	Leaves and stems, essence
Planet:	Venus
Element:	Air
Magical uses:	Clairvoyance, compassion, confidence, consecration, contact other planes, courage, divination, love, magic, meditation, money, prevent nightmares, protection, psychic development & growth
Recipe:	2¹/₂, ¹/₄, ¹/₈ 1¹/₂ Water
Scent:	Bittersweet, herby, fiery

Care should be taken when using thyme essence as it has been known to cause minor skin irritation in some people.

Turmeric
Curcuma Longa

Common names:	Curcuma, Zedoary
Part used:	Root
Planet:	Mars
Element:	Fire
Magical uses:	Aphrodisiac, commanding, confidence, courage, exorcism, magic, passion, sensuality, spell-breaking, strength
Recipe:	1½, 1, ⅛, 2 Water
Scent:	Strong, fiery, spicy, peppery

Because of its fiery essence, turmeric is an excellent and preferred substitute in recipes that call for the use of pepper.

Uva Ursi
Arctostaphylos Uva-ursi

Common names:	Bearberry
Part used:	Leaves
Planet:	Saturn
Element:	Earth
Magical uses:	Animals, protection, strength
Recipe:	1½, 1, ⅛, 1½ FW
Scent:	Autumn leaves, herby, hint of pine

Valerian
Valeriana Officinalis

Common names:	All-heal, Amantilla, Blessed Herb, Capon's Tail, Garden Heliotrope, Phu, St. George's Herb, Setwell, Vandal Root
Part used:	Root, essence
Planet:	Mercury
Element:	Earth
Magical uses:	Animals, aphrodisiac, consecration, exorcism, harmony, love, magic, overcome opposition, peace, psychic protection, spell-breaking, tranquility
Recipe:	1, $1^1/_2$, $^1/_8$, 2 Water
Scent:	Sour, tart, chemical-like

Vervain
Verbena Officinalis

Common names:	Blue Vervain, Enchanter's Plant, Herb of Grace, Holy Herb, Juno's Tears, Van Van
Part used:	Leaves and stems, essence
Planet:	Venus
Element:	Earth
Magical uses:	Aphrodisiac, consecration, creativity, inspiration, knowledge, love, magic, material objects, to prevent nightmares, prosperity, protection, success, transformation
Recipe:	$2^1/_2$, $^1/_4$, $^1/_8$, $1^1/_2$ Water
Scent:	Bitter, strong, penetrating

Vetiver
Vetiveria Zizanioides

Common names:	Khus Khus, Vetevert
Part used:	Root, essence
Planet:	Venus
Element:	Earth
Magical uses:	Commanding, good luck, to increase power of spells, love, protection, psychic protection, success, virility
Recipe:	2½, 0, ⅛, 1½ Water
Scent:	Woody, sweet, hint of bitter grass

Violet
Viola Odorata

Common name:	None
Part used:	Essence
Planet:	Venus
Element:	Air
Magical uses:	Aphrodisiac, beauty, contact other planes, fidelity, gentleness, good luck, harmony, honesty, love, modesty, peace, tranquility, transformation
Scent:	Gentle, subtle, hint of flowers

When using violet essence, care should be taken as it can cause minor skin irritation or rashes.

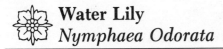

Water Lily
Nymphaea Odorata

Common names:	Cow Cabbage, Water Nymph, Yon
Part used:	Root, essence
Planet:	Moon
Element:	Water
Magical uses:	Animals, anti-aphrodisiac, beauty, endings, release, renewal.
Recipe:	1½, 1, ⅛, 1¾ Water
Scent:	Tart, earthy, muddy

Willow
Salix

Common names:	Arovous, Osier, Saille, Tree of Enchantment, Weeping Willow, Witches' Asprin
Part used:	Bark
Planet:	Moon
Element:	Water
Magical uses:	Clairvoyance, compassion, consecration, determination, divination, endings, exorcism, gentleness, love, magic, to prevent nightmares, to prevent theft, release, spell-breaking
Recipe:	2½, 0, ⅛, 1¾ Water
Scent:	Slight hint of woody sweetness

Wintergreen
Gaulteria Procumbeus

Common names:	Boxberry, Checkerberry, Deerberry, Gaulteria, Mountain Tea, Spice Berry, Teaberry
Part used:	Leaves, essence
Planet:	Mercury
Element:	Earth
Magical uses:	Animals, contact other planes, good luck, money
Recipe:	$2^1/_2$, $^1/_4$, $^1/_8$, $1^3/_4$ Water
Scent:	Mild, woody, hint of pine

To get the sweet tasty scent of wintergreen, you must use essence. Although it is widely used in food and beverages, wintergreen should be handled carefully. Externally, it can cause irritation of the skin and mucous membranes. Taken internally, it is very toxic and can even lead to death.

Wisteria
Wisteria Chinensis

Common name:	Caspar's Flower, Tungnamu
Part used:	Essence
Planet:	Venus
Element:	Air
Magical uses:	Contact other planes, gentleness, inspiration, knowledge, love, protection, psychic development & growth, wisdom
Scent:	Strong, flowery, unusual

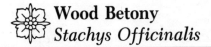

Wood Betony
Stachys Officinalis

Common names:	Betony, Bishopwort
Part used:	Leaves
Planet:	Jupiter
Element:	Fire
Magical uses:	Consecration, to prevent intoxication, protection, psychic protection
Recipe:	$2^{1}/_{2}$, $^{1}/_{4}$, $^{1}/_{8}$, $1^{3}/_{4}$ Water
Scent:	Tart, woody, herby

Woodruff
Asperula Odorata

Common names:	Herb Walter, Master of the Wood, Wood Musk
Part used:	Leaves and stems
Planet:	Mars
Element:	Fire
Magical uses:	Commanding, consecration, endings, magic, overcome opposition, protection, psychic protection, release, renewal, success, transformation
Recipe:	$2^{1}/_{2}$, $^{1}/_{4}$, $^{1}/_{8}$, $2^{1}/_{4}$ Water
Scent:	Tart, bitter, musky, earthy

Wood Sorrel
Oxalis Corniculata/Oxalis Acetosella

Common names:	Fairy Bells, Oxalis, Seamsog, Sourgrass, Wood Shamrock
Part used:	Leaves and stems
Planet:	Saturn
Element:	Earth
Magical uses:	Good luck, love, magic, to overcome opposition, psychic protection
Recipe:	2, $1/2$, $1/8$, $1 1/4$ QB
Scent:	Tart, bitter, sour

Wormwood
Artemisia Absinthium

Common names:	Absinthe, Artemisia, Green Ginger, Old Woman
Part used:	Leaves and stems
Planet:	Mars
Element:	Fire
Magical uses:	Animals, aphrodisiac, clairvoyance, contact other planes, determination, divination, exorcism, love, magic, to overcome opposition, protection, psychic development & growth, spell-breaking, transformation
Recipe:	$2 1/2$, $1/4$, $1/8$, $1 1/2$ Water
Scent:	Bitter-herb, woody, "cattails"

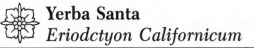

Yarrow
Achillea Millfolium

Common names:	Arrow Root, Bloodwort, Carpenter's Weed, Death Flower, Devil's Nettle, Dog Daisy, Gearwe, Milfoil, Old Man's Pepper, Sanguinary, Thousand Leaf, Woundwort
Part used:	Leaves and stems
Planet:	Saturn
Element:	Earth
Magical uses:	Animals, clairvoyance, consecration, contact other planes, divination, endings, exorcism, fertility, good luck, to increase power of spells, longevity, love, magic, protection, psychic protection, release, spell-breaking, weddings
Recipe:	2¹/₂, ¹/₄, ¹/₈, 1³/₄ QB
Scent:	Semisweet, grassy, mild

Yerba Santa
Eriodctyon Californicum

Common names:	Bearsweed, Consumptive's Weed, Gum Bush, Holy Herb, Mountain Balm, Tarweed
Part used:	Leaves
Planet:	Saturn
Element:	Earth
Magical uses:	Animals, exorcism, protection, psychic development & growth, spell-breaking, strength
Recipe:	2¹/₂, ¹/₂, ¹/₈, 1³/₄ FW
Scent:	Dry, mild, hint of wood, spice and herbs

Yew
Taxus Baccata/Taxus Canadensis

Common name:	Chinwood
Part used:	Needles
Planet:	Saturn
Element:	Earth
Magical uses:	Clairvoyance, compassion, consolation, divination, memory, peace of mind, protection
Recipe:	2, 1/2, 1/8, 1 1/2 FW
Scent:	Subtle yet penetrating, hint of cedar and herbs

Yew is very toxic. If taken internally, it can cause trembling, difficulty in breathing, stoppage of heartbeats, and even death.

Yohimbe
Coryanthe Yohimbine

Common name:	Black Aphrodite, Passion Bark
Part used:	Bark
Planet:	Venus
Element:	Earth
Magical uses:	Aphrodisiac, commanding, to increase power of spells, love, passion, sensuality
Recipe:	2 1/2, 1/4, 1/8, 2, Water
Scent:	Dark, earthy, exotic, sensuous

Part
Three

Incense
Recipes

MUNDANE INCENSE

As your knowledge and skill in using incense increases, you will eventually realize that there is sometimes more to incense than just a nice fragrance. Later we will discuss the magical, ritual, and astrological uses of incense. For the time being, however, fragrance should be all that you are concerned with. This section is devoted to just that.

Before making one of these recipes, you may want to read the description of each herb in the Herbal, so you will know which parts of the herb to use. When you use these recipes, please note that I have not included measuring units. All the recipes are made to be used with a teaspoon (or fraction thereof) as the unit of measure. If you want to increase or decrease your recipes, use Appendices 2 and 3 on pages 245 and 249 for adjustments. Also, if you cannot remember the recipe for the bonding agents I cite as QB, FW or LF, please turn back to page 14 for instructions.

You'll note that some recipes have two or more versions. If one doesn't work for you, try another!

African

Yohimbe 1	Musk Root $1/2$
Frankincense $1/2$	Aloes $1/8$
Acacia 1	QB $1^1/2$

Aphrodite

Damiana 1/2   Musk Root 1/4
Yohimbe 1/2   Saw Palmetto 1/4
Rose 1   Jasmine 1/2
Rose Oil   Jasmine Oil
Musk Oil   QB 1 1/2

Applesauce

Cinnamon 3/4   Sandalwood 1/2
Camomile 1 3/4   QB 1 1/2

Arabian

Frankincense 1/4   Cassia 1/4
Cascarilla 1   Musk Root 1/4
Benzoin 1/4   Sandalwood 3/4
Cloves 1/4   Musk Oil
LF 1 1/2

Bible (Loose only)

Mugwort 1/2   Benzoin 1/2
Basil 1/4   Lily of the Valley 1/2
Solomon's Seal 1/2   Frankincense 1/2
Primrose 1/2   Lily of the Valley Oil
Jalap 1/4

Blodeuwedd

Locust 1/2
Oak 1/4
Nettle 1/4
Meadowsweet 1/4
Primrose 1/4
Lady's Mantle 1/4

Maidenhair 1/2
Rose 1
Red Clover 1/4
Burdock 1/4
Melilot 1/2
LF 2

Cernunnos

Pine 1
Frankincense 1/4
Oak 1/4
Bay 1/2
Wormwood 1/4
QB 1 1/2

Patchouli 1/4
Musk Root 1/4
Cinnamon 1/2
Pine Oil
Musk Oil

Cinnamon & Rose #1

Sandalwood 1 1/2
Cinnamon 3/4
Water 2

Rose 3/4
Rose Oil

Cinnamon & Rose #2

Rose 1
Cedar 1/2
Rosemary 1/4
QB 1 3/4

Cinnamon 1/2
Sandalwood 1
Rose Oil

Cleopatra

Pine 1/2
Sandalwood 1
Orris 1/4
Patchouli 1/4
Myrrh 1/4
FW 2

Musk Root 1/4
Frankincense 1/4
Rose 1/2
Cinnamon 1/4
Rose Oil

Egyptian

Frankincense 1/2
Sandalwood 1
Acacia 1/2
Myrrh 1/4
Juniper 1/4
LF 2

Henna 1/4
Spikenard 1/4
Onion 1/4
Cinnamon 1/2
Cedar 1/2

Egyptian Sun*

Benzoin 1/2
Sunflower 1/2
Lotus Root 1/2
Cinnamon 1/2
FW 1 1/2

Frankincense 1/2
Sandalwood 1/2
Frankincense Oil
Cinnamon Oil

Evergreen Spice #1

Hemlock 2 1/2
FW 1 1/2

Cinnamon 1/2

Evergreen Spice #2

Cinnamon 1/2
Pine Oil

Pine 2 1/2
QB 1 1/2

Evergreen Spice #3

Cedar 1
Cloves 1/2

Sandalwood 1
Water 1 1/2

Evergreen Spice #4

Pine 1
Hemlock 1/2
Sassafras 1/2
Pine Oil (optional)

Cedar 1/2
Cloves 1/4
Clove Oil
QB 11/2

Five Saints

Valerian 1/4
   (St. George's Herb)
Basil 1
   (St. Josephswort)
Mugwort 1/2
   (St. John's Plant)

St. Johnswort 1
Solomon's Seal 1/2
   (St. Mary's Seal)
QB 13/4

Forest Flower #1

Sandalwood 11/2
Benzoin 1/2
Cascarilla 1/2
QB 2

Cloves 1/2
Eucalyptus 1/4
Eucalyptus Oil

Forest Flower #2

Sandalwood 1
Benzoin 1/2
Cascarilla 1/4
Myrrh 1/4

Cloves 1/4
Cinnamon 1/2
Lavender 1/4
FW 1 3/4

Frankincense Blend #1

Frankincense 1/4
Cinnamon 1/2
Lavender 1

Rosemary 1
Sandalwood 1/2
FW 1 1/2

Frankincense Blend #2

Frankincense 1/4
Benzoin 1/4
Orris 1/4
Cascarilla 1/2
FW 1 1/2

Cinnamon 1/2
Rose 1
Sandalwood 1/2
Rose Oil

Frankincense Blend (Loose only) #3

Frankincense 1/2
Benzoin 1/4
Lavender 1
Patchouli 1/4

Cloves 1/4
Rose 1
Sandalwood 1/2

Guardian Angel (Loose only)

Angelica 1/4   Yerba Santa 1/4
Valerian 1/8   Vervain 1/2
Cascara Sagrada 11/4   Frankincense 1/2

Hindu

Basil 3/4   Frankincense 1/4
Sandalwood 1   Cinnamon 1/4
Pomegranate 1/2   Jasmine Oil
Jasmine 1/2   Water 2

Icicles

Sandalwood 21/2   Menthol 1/8
Camphor 1/4   Eucalyptus Oil
Benzoin 1/4   Wintergreen Oil
Water 13/4

Imperial China

Cassia 1/2   Ginseng 1/8
Cloves 1/2   Musk Root 1/4
Patchouli 1/4   Sandalwood 1
Myrrh 1/8   Water 13/4

Indian Meditation

Sandalwood $1^1/_2$
Rose 1
Cinnamon $^1/_2$

Camphor $^1/_4$
Rose Oil
Water $1^3/_4$

Indian Raja

Cinnamon $^3/_4$
Sandalwood $1^1/_4$
Cloves $^1/_4$
Musk Oil
QB $1^3/_4$

Musk Root $^1/_4$
Benzoin $^1/_4$
Curry $^1/_4$
Jasmine Oil

Isis

Vetiver 1
Myrrh $^1/_4$
Frankincense $^1/_4$
Musk Root $^1/_2$
Civit Oil
LF $1^1/_2$

Myrtle $^1/_2$
Cassia $^1/_2$
Sandalwood $^1/_2$
Musk Oil
Bayberry Oil

Japanese

Star Anise $^3/_4$
Cassia $^3/_4$
Water $1^3/_4$

Sandalwood 1
Cherry Oil

Lavender & Rose

Benzoin 1/4
Lavender 1
Cinnamon 1/2
QB 1 1/2

Rose 1
Patchouli 1/4
Sandalwood 1/4

Leo's Delight

Lavender 1 1/4
Frankincense 1/2
Cinnamon 1/2
QB 1 3/4

Bay 1/2
Menthol 1/8
Sandalwood 1/2

Magickal Mystery Tour

Bay 3/4
Frankincense 1/4
Sandalwood 1 1/4
QB 1 3/4

Cinnamon 1/2
Dragon's Blood 1/4
Lilac Oil

Mexican

Saw Palmetto 1
Damiana 1 1/2
Sarsaparilla 1/2

Copal 1/4
Cactus Flower Oil
QB 1 1/2

Nine Herbs

Fennel $1/4$
Camomile $1/2$
Thyme $1/2$
Wormwood $1/4$
Parsley $1/4$

Wood Betony $1/2$
Plantain $1/4$
Nettle $1/4$
Elder $1/4$
Water $1 1/4$

Pan

Sage $1/2$
Bay $1/2$
Pine 1
Cinquefoil $1/4$
Musk Oil

Patchouli $1/4$
Musk Root $1/2$
Cedar $1/2$
Pine Oil
Water $1 3/4$

Persian Flower

Sandalwood $1 3/4$
Musk Root $1/2$
Frankincense $1/2$
Myrrh $1/4$
QB $1 3/4$

Cinnamon $1/4$
Jasmine $1/4$
Musk Oil
Jasmine Oil

Pertunda

Red Sandalwood 1	Musk Root $3/4$
Lavender $3/4$	Rose $3/4$
Orchid Oil	Strawberry Oil
Rose Oil	Water $1^1/2$

Roman Sun (Loose only)*

Sunflower 1	Cloves $1/2$
Safflower $1/2$	Myrrh $1/2$
Frankincense $1/2$	Heliotrope Oil
Cinnamon 1	

Suburbia

Rose $1^1/2$	Red Clover $1/2$
Crabgrass 1	Rose Oil
QB $1^1/2$	

Tibetan Temple

Frankincense $1/4$	Cinnamon $1/4$
Juniper $1/2$	Patchouli $1/4$
Sandalwood $1^1/4$	Cedar $1/2$
FW $1^1/2$	

Utnapishtim

Cedar 1 1/4
Myrtle 1 1/4

Bayberry Oil
FW 1 1/4

Virgin Mary

Rosemary 1
Marigold 1/2
Primrose 1/2
Solomon's Seal 1

Lily of the Valley 1/2
Lily of the Valley Oil
Spearmint Oil
QB 1 1/2

Winter King

Pine 1
Hemlock 3/4
Bay 1/2
LF 1 1/4

Holly 1/4
Mistletoe 1/4
Wintergreen Oil

Yule Incense (Loose only)

Myrrh 1/4
Frankincense 1/2
Benzoin 1/2

Sandalwood 1 1/2
Bayberry Oil

MAGICAL INCENSE

There is a vast difference of opinion over just what magic is, or for that matter, if magic actually exists. Numerous books have been written on the subject, so I will not delve too deeply into the mechanics of magic here.

What is magic? To a person seeing a TV or hearing a radio for the first time, this is magic of the highest order. To us, however, radios and televisions are commonplace. To those who know and use it, magic is just a tool. Like any ordinary tool, such as a hammer or screwdriver, it is neither good nor evil. Its function and purpose is entirely in the hands of the user. This is where the main problem of using magic lies. If you don't know how to use a hammer properly, you may end up hitting your thumb with it. The same thing can happen when using a psychic tool such as magic. A magical rite done with the best of intentions can have disastrous results if performed by an amateur.

Before going any further, let me say a few things to those of you who may be a little skeptical about magic. Be patient, keep an open mind, and always remember that with the proper motivation and enough perseverance nothing is impossible.

To the doubting Thomas (and Thomasina), the best definition of magic I can give you is that it is the art and science of increasing the rate of coincidence. When working magic, the word coincidence seems to pop up continually. As long as the desired results are obtained, it doesn't really matter if they come about by way of magic or coincidence.

If you really want to work magic, there are a few things that you should know and do before you even start. The following is a brief listing of some of the things you should be aware of when you work magic. It is a sort of "psychic etiquette code."

• First, and most important of all, study and learn everything you can on the subject. Know exactly what you are doing before you attempt to do it.

• When using someone else's rite, always follow the procedures step-by-step. Never take short-cuts or ignore instructions.

• Start small; do only minor magical operations at first. Once you have mastered these, then and only then should you move on to something more complex.

• Never do or use anything that will endanger anyone's health or well-being, either in the material world or on other planes. Such actions are spiritually, morally, and ethically wrong, and will always return, in one form or another, to the sender (you).

• Don't depend entirely on magic to achieve your goal. If you want something, you must work to get it. The effort you put out to reach your goal matters the most; magic just gives things a little "push" in the right direction.

• Magic is a tool, but belief is the hand that uses it. You've got to believe in what you're doing, and in yourself, in order for magic to work. If you treat magic as a game or a new fad to try out, then that's what it will become. If you don't truly believe, then your rites will all fail miserably.

I could go on and on, but then this would be a book on magic instead of incense. Magic is an interesting, absorbing, and complex subject. Once you have begun to work magic, the following recipes may be of use to you. They are just a small sampling of recipes for several different magical operations.

Included in this section are several recipes for working with animals. Let me repeat what I've already stated: I do not advocate or condone the misuse or maltreatment of any living thing. The animal recipes in this section are designed to promote positive interactions with animals. Such actions include the healing of sick or injured animals, protection of or from animals, soothing and calming of distraught or frightened animals, creating a bond of friendship with an animal, and attracting animal familiars.

As you progress in your magical studies, you will probably want to invent your own recipes. To assist you in doing so, I have included a listing of herbs for each magical operation in Appendix 6 at the back of the book.

The following recipes are designed to be used in cone form, but can usually be adapted for use in cylinder or stick incense. By eliminating the base, tragacanth, and liquid, they can also be used as loose incense.

All measurements in these recipes are in teaspoons (or fractions thereof). If you want to increase or decrease the recipes, please turn to the conversion tables Appendices 2 and 3 on pages 245 and 249. Also note: if you cannot remember the recipes for the bonding agents (QB, FW, and LF) please turn back to page 14.

Animals

Catnip $1^1/_2$	Pine $1^1/_2$
Frankincense $^1/_4$	QB $1^1/_4$

Animals — Cats

Catnip $1^1/_2$	Ground Ivy $^1/_2$
Life Everlasting $^1/_2$	Water $1^1/_2$

Animals — Dogs

Dogwood 3	Burdock $^1/_2$
Yarrow $^1/_2$	QB $1^3/_4$

Animals — Fowl

Chickweed 1/2
Mistletoe 1/2
Valerian 1/8
QB 2

Cranesbill 1/2
Sandalwood 1
Mandrake 1/4

Animals — Fowl

Plantain 1/2
Mandrake 1/2
Reed 1/2

Spikenard 1/2
Sandalwood 1
Water 1 3/4

Animals — Hooved

Water Lily 1/4
Wintergreen 1/4
Deer's Tongue 1/2
Coltsfoot 1/2
Honeysuckle 1/4
QB 1 3/4

St. Johnswort 1/2
Melilot 1/2
Elecampane 1/4
Wintergreen oil
Spearmint oil

Animals — Serpents #1 (Loose only)

Chickweed 1/2
Plantain 1

Dragon's Blood 1
Tarragon 1

Animals — Serpents #2 (Loose only)

Juniper 1/2   Marjoram 2
Plantain 1

Animals — Wild

Uva Ursi 1/2   Motherwort 1/2
Yerba Santa 1/4   Lady's Mantle 1/2
Burdock 1/4   Dandelion 1/2
QB 1 1/2

Animals — Wild & Hooved

Deer's Tongue 1/2   Sandalwood 1 1/2
Musk Root 1/2   Musk Oil
Water 1 1/2

Anti-Aphrodisiac

Rue 1/2   Menthol 1/4
Water Lily 1/2   Lavender 1 3/4
Water 1 1/2

Attract a Lover #1

Lovage 1   Patchouli $1/4$
Orris $1/2$ Lemon Verbena Oil
Lemon Verbena 1   FW $13/4$

Attract a Lover #2 (Loose only)

Cloves $1/2$ Musk Root $1/2$
Rose 1   Red Sandalwood $1/2$
Saw Palmetto $1/4$ Rose Oil
Juniper $1/2$ Musk Oil

Beauty #1

Angelica $1/2$ Cherry 1
Elder 1   Strawberry oil
Musk Root $3/4$ FW $13/4$

Beauty #2

Rose 1   Lady's Mantle $1/2$
Maidenhair $1/2$ Rose Oil
Linden $3/4$ QB $11/4$

Break Off an Affair #1

Camphor $1/4$ Pennyroyal $1 1/2$
Slippery Elm 1   FW $1 1/2$

Break Off an Affair #2

Menthol $1/4$ Lavender $1 1/2$
Willow $1 1/2$ Water $1 3/4$

Cold

Cloves $1/2$ Menthol $1/8$
Juniper $1/4$ Eucalyptus Oil
Willow 2   Wintergreen Oil
Water $1 3/4$

Cold #2

Pine $1 1/4$ Camphor $1/8$
Hemlock $1 1/4$ Menthol $1/8$
Cedar $1/2$ Pine Oil
QB $1 1/2$

Commanding #1

Elder ¹/₄
Spikenard ¹/₂
Slippery Elm ¹/₄
St. Johnswort 1

Musk Root ¹/₂
Patchouli ¹/₄
Musk Oil
LF 1¹/₂

Commanding #2

Vetiver 1¹/₄
Calamus 1
Water 1¹/₂

Musk Root ¹/₂
Safflower ¹/₂

Commanding #3 (Loose only)

Safflower 1
Catnip ³/₄

Poppy ¹/₂
Marigold 1

Compassion #1

Allspice ¹/₂
Myrtle 2

Bayberry Oil
QB 1³/₄

Compassion #2

Allspice $1/2$
Rue $1/4$
Rose Oil
QB $1^1/2$

Pine $1^1/2$
Rose $1/2$
Pine Oil

Compassion #3

Elder $1/4$
Poppy $1/4$
Lemon Balm 1

Willow 1
Lemon Balm Oil
FW $1^1/2$

Conceive a Child

Mistletoe $1/2$
Mandrake 1
FW $1^3/4$

Motherwort $1^1/2$
Strawberry Oil

Confidence #1

Rosemary 1
Musk Root 1
QB $1^1/4$

Garlic $1/2$
Camomile $1/4$

Confidence #2

St. Johnswort 1
Thyme 1
Water 1½

Oak ½
Woodruff ¼

Contact Other Planes #1

Frankincense ¼
Acacia ¼
Star Anise ½
QB 1½

Thyme ½
Oak Moss ¼
Sandalwood 1

Contact Other Planes #2

Frankincense ¼
Angelica ¼
Patchouli ¼
Mistletoe ¼

Dittany 1
Sandalwood ½
Wisteria Oil
QB 1½

Defeat an Enemy

St. Johnswort 1
Woodruff ½
Oak ½

Onion ¼
Rosemary ¾
FW 1½

Determination #1

Althea $1/2$
Camomile $1/2$
Oak $1/2$

Thyme 1
Garlic $1/4$
QB $1^1/4$

Determination # 2

Rosemary 1
Willow 1
Water $1^3/4$

Musk Root 1
Musk Oil

Determination #3

Allspice $1/2$
St. Johnswort $1^1/4$
Water $2^1/4$

Southernwood $1/2$
Willow $3/4$

Dispel "Catty Ways"*

Catnip 1
Dragon's Blood 1

Sandalwood 1
QB $1^1/2$

Divination #1

St. Johnswort 1
Wormwood 3/4
QB 1 1/2

Bay 3/4
Frankincense 1/2

Divination #2

Dittany 1
Damiana 1/2
Orris 1/2

Camphor 1/4
Solomon's Seal 1/4
QB 1 1/2

Divination #3

Rosemary 1
Parsley 1/4
Bay 1/2

Dittany 1
Pomegranate 1/2
Water 1 3/4

Divination #4

Cinquefoil 3/4
Valerian 1/4
Deer's Tongue 1/2

Frankincense 1/2
Sandalwood 1
QB 2

Divination #5

Cinnamon 1/2
Chickweed 1/2
Water 2

Thyme 1
Sandalwood 1

Divination #6

Yarrow 1
St. Johnswort 1
QB 1 3/4

Frankincense 1/4
Bay 1/2

Divination #7

Lavender 1
Rose 1
QB 1 1/2

Star Anise 1/2
Sandalwood 1/2

Divination #8

Dittany 1
Acacia 3/4
QB 1 3/4

Cinquefoil 3/4
Clary Sage 1

Divination #9

St. Johnswort $1/2$
Dittany 1
Frankincense $1/4$
LF $13/4$

Bay $1/2$
Rosemary $1/2$
Sandalwood $1/2$

Divine Intervention (Loose only)

Dragon's Blood $1/2$
Frankincense $1/2$
Angelica $1/4$
Galangal $3/4$

Bay $1/2$
Sandalwood $1/2$
Cinnamon $1/4$

Divorce #1 (Loose only)

Frankincense $1/2$
Rue $1/2$
Allspice $1/2$
Marjoram $1/4$

Pennyroyal $3/4$
Yarrow $1/2$
Menthol $1/8$
Sandalwood $1/2$

Divorce #2 (Loose only)

Frankincense $1/2$
Cloves $1/2$
Melilot 1

Slippery Elm $1/2$
Comfrey $1/4$

Domestic Tranquility

Sage $3/4$
Ground Ivy $1/2$
Linden $1 1/4$
Water 2

Rue $1/4$
Bayberry $1/4$
Bayberry Oil

Ease Emotional Pain (Loose only)

Bay 3
Allspice $3/4$

Dragon's Blood $1/4$
Storax $3/4$

End Negativity & Give Hope #1

Dittany 1
Camomile $1/2$
QB $1 1/4$

Melilot $3/4$
Patchouli $1/4$

End Negativity & Give Hope #2

Thyme 1
Rue $1/2$
Water $1 1/2$

Woodruff $1/2$
Cloves $1/2$

End Negativity & Give Hope #3

Dittany 1^1/$_2$ Rue ^{1}/$_4$
Burdock ^{1}/$_2$ Patchouli ^{1}/$_4$
QB 1^1/$_2$

End Nightmares #1

Thyme 1   Camomile 1
Willow 1   Water 1^3/$_4$

End Nightmares #2

Star Anise ^{1}/$_4$ Willow 1
Lemon Verbena ^{3}/$_4$ Lemon Verbena Oil
Thyme ^{3}/$_4$ Water 1^3/$_4$

Exorcism #1

St. Johnswort 1^1/$_4$ Yarrow ^{1}/$_2$
Bay ^{1}/$_2$ Onion ^{1}/$_4$
QB 1^1/$_2$

Exorcism #2 (Loose only)

Asafoetida 1/8   Angelica 1/2
Benzoin 1/2   St. Johnswort 1/2
Frankincense 1/2   Cascara Sagrada 1/2

Exorcism #3

Wormwood 1   Orris 1/2
Cascara Sagrada 1   Solomon's Seal 1/2
QB 1 3/4

Exorcism #4

St. Johnswort 1   Frankincense 1/4
Wormwood 1/2   Angelica 1/2
Bay 1/2   QB 1 1/2

Exorcism #5 (Loose only)

Basil 1/2   Nettle 1/4
Rosemary 1/2   Frankincense 1/2
Garlic 1/4   Willow 1

Fertility #1

Star Anise $1/2$
Mandrake $1/4$
Pomegranate $1/2$
Poppy $1/4$

Mistletoe $1/4$
Cherry $3/4$
Allspice $1/4$
LF $1^{1}/2$

Fertility #2

Basil $1/2$
Dragon's Blood $1/2$
Holly $1/4$
LF $1^{1}/2$

Pine 1
Juniper $1/4$
Base $1/2$

Fertility #3

Allspice $1/2$
Cherry 1
Saw Palmetto $1/4$
Strawberry $1/4$
FW $1^{1}/2$

Blueberry $1/4$
Yarrow $1/2$
Cucumber $1/4$
Strawberry Oil

Fidelity

Basil $1/4$
Dragon's Blood $1/4$
Red Sandalwood 1
QB $1^{1}/2$

Rosemary $1/2$
Dogwood 1
Honeysuckle Oil

Friendship (Loose only)

Acacia $\frac{1}{2}$ Frankincense $\frac{1}{2}$
Rosemary 1   Dogwood 1
Elder $\frac{1}{4}$

Gain #1 (Loose only)

Star Anise $\frac{1}{2}$ Juniper $\frac{1}{2}$
Poppy $\frac{1}{4}$ Cherry 1
Mistletoe $\frac{1}{2}$

Gain #2

Cucumber $\frac{1}{4}$ Saw Palmetto $\frac{1}{4}$
Allspice $\frac{3}{4}$ Marigold $\frac{1}{2}$
Sunflower 1   FW $1\frac{1}{4}$

Gentleness #1

Willow $1\frac{1}{2}$ Henna $\frac{1}{2}$
Lemon Balm $\frac{1}{2}$ Lavender $\frac{1}{2}$
Meadowsweet $\frac{1}{4}$ Lilac Oil
QB 2

Gentleness #2

Lavender 1
Camomile 1/4
Lady's Mantle 1/4
Maidenhair 1/4

Motherwort 1/4
Willow 3/4
Wisteria Oil
Water 1 1/2

Good Luck #1

Dragon's Blood 1/2
Mistletoe 1/2
LF 1 1/2

Cascara Sagrada 1
Linden 1

Good Luck #2 (Loose only)

Cinnamon 1/2
Angelica 1/4
Camomile 1/2

Myrrh 1/4
Red Clover 1
Sandalwood 1/2

Good Luck #3

Musk Root 1/2
Rose 1 1/2
Red Clover 1/2

Galangal 1/2
Rose Oil
QB 1 1/2

Good Luck #4 (Loose only)

Rosemary 1   Sandalwood 1/2
Dragon's blood 1/2   Rose Oil
Musk Root 1/2   Musk Oil
Rose 3/4

Happiness #1

Myrrh 1/4   Sandalwood 3/4
Marjoram 1/4   Oregano 3/4
Dittany 1   Spearmint Oil
LF 11/2

Happiness #2

Oregano 1   Marigold 1
Rosemary 1   FW 11/2

Home Protection #1

Orris Root 1   Patchouli 1/4
Sandalwood 1   Cloves 1/4
Lavender 1/2   FW 13/4

Home Protection #2 (Loose only)

Frankincense $1/2$

Sage $3/4$

Basil $1/2$

Mistletoe $1/2$

Garlic $1/2$

Rosemary $3/4$

Spearmint Oil

Rue $1/2$

Sandalwood 1

Myrrh $1/2$

Orris $1/2$

Mandrake $1/2$

Yarrow $1/2$

This recipe is also known as "Witches Bottle."

Keep Secret #1

Dogwood $1^{1}/4$

Life Everlasting $1/2$

Lavender $1/2$

Honeysuckle Oil

Ground Ivy $1/2$

Rose $1/2$

Rose Oil

Water 2

Keep Secret #2

Dogwood 1

Sage $1/2$

Pomegranate $1/2$

QB $1^{3}/4$

Tarragon $1/4$

Juniper $1/4$

Lavender $1/2$

Knowledge & Wisdom #1

Angelica ¹/₄
Vervain ¹/₄
Cinnamon ³/₄

Sage 1
Solomon's Seal ¹/₂
QB 1¹/₂

Knowledge & Wisdom #2

Solomon's Seal 1
Benzoin ¹/₄
Vervain ¹/₂
LF 1¹/₂

Cloves ¹/₂
Bay ¹/₂
Wisteria Oil

Law #1

Cascara Sagrada 1¹/₂
Galangal 1

Jalap ¹/₂
QB 2

Law #2

Cascara Sagrada 1¹/₄
Scammony ¹/₂
Water 2

Sandalwood 1
Onion ¹/₄

Love #1

Rose 1¼   Red Sandalwood 1
Musk Root ¼   Cinnamon ½
Patchouli ¼   Rose Oil
Musk Oil   QB 1½

Love #2

Lavender 1   Rose ½
Rosemary 1   QB 1¼

Love #3

Benzoin ½   Patchouli ¼
Jasmine ¼   Musk Root½
Rose 1   Sandalwood ½
Musk Oil   Rose Oil
Civit Oil   Jasmine Oil
QB 1½

Love #4

Rose 1½   Red Sandalwood ½
Cinnamon ½   Rose Oil
Deer's Tongue ½   QB 1½

Magic #1 (Loose only)

Frankincense 1/2
St. Johnswort 1/2
Willow 1
Dragon's Blood 1/2
Salep 1/4

Vervain 1/2
Cinquefoil 1/2
Patchouli 1/4
Bay 1/2

Magic #2

Bay 1/2
Dittany 1
Storax 1/4
FW 1 1/2

Frankincense 1/2
Cinnamon 1/2
Willow 1

Meditation #1

Parsley 1/4
Sage 1/2
Rosemary 1/2
QB 1 1/2

Thyme 1/2
Dittany 1
Bay 1/2

Meditation #2 (Loose only)

Camomile 3/4
Rosemary 1

Frankincense 1/2
Cinnamon 3/4

Memory #1

Lavender 1
Life Everlasting 1/4
Marigold 1/2
QB 11/2

Rosemary 1/2
Honeysuckle 1/2
Honeysuckle Oil

Memory #2

Bay 1/2
Benzoin 1/4
QB 11/2

Cloves 1/2
Rosemary 11/2

Memory #3

Benzoin 1/4
Marigold 3/4
Rose Oil
QB 11/2

Rose 1
Lavender 1
Lavender Oil

Modesty

Willow 11/4
Broom 1/2
Lilac Oil
QB 11/2

Camomile 1/2
Lily of the Valley 1/2
Lily of the Valley Oil

Money #1

Basil 1
Cinquefoil 1
Galangal $1/2$

Hyssop $1/2$
Base $1/2$
LF $13/4$

Money #2 (Loose only)

Cinnamon $3/4$
Cascara Sagrada $11/4$

Dragon's Blood $1/2$
Salep $1/2$

Money #3 (Loose only)

Lavender $11/4$
Camomile $1/4$
Acacia $1/4$

Comfrey $1/4$
Red Clover 1

Money #4

Lovage 1
Bay 1
FW $11/2$

Jalap $1/4$
Meadowsweet $1/2$

Money #5

Thyme 1¼   Spikenard ½
Red Clover 1   Nutmeg ¼
QB 1½

Overcome Opposition #1

Bay ½   Oak ½
Red Clover 1   St. Johnswort ¾
QB 1½

Overcome Opposition #2

Cloves ¾   Woodruff ½
Garlic ½   Red Clover ½
Jalap ¼   QB 1¼

Passion #1

Cascarilla 1¼   Savory ½
Cranesbill ½   Civit Oil
Musk Root ½   Water 1¾

Passion #2

Yohimbe 3/4
Ginger 1/4
Damiana 2 1/2

Cinnamon 1/2
Ambergris Oil
Water 1 1/2

Peaceful Home (Loose only) †

Frankincense 1
Rose 1/2
Lavender 1/2

Rose Oil
Clove Oil

Peace & Protection

Lavender 1
Thyme 3/4
Basic 3/4
Vervain 1/4

Frankincense 1/4
Rue 1/4
Benzoin 1/4
QB 1 1/2

Physical Love #1

Cascarilla 3/4
Damiana 3/4
Yohimbe 1/2
Water 1 1/2

Musk Root 1/2
Bergamot Oil
Ambergris Oil

Physical Love #2

Cranesbill ¼
Savory ¾
Ginger ¼
Mandrake ½

Cascarilla 1
Jasmine Oil
Civit Oil
LF 1¾

Prevent Theft #1

Ground Ivy 1
Rosemary 1½

Juniper ½
QB 1½

Prevent Theft #2

Dogwood ½
Caraway ¼
Rosemary ½
QB 1½

Tarragon ¼
Willow 1
Honeysuckle Oil

Prophetic Dreams

Mugwort ½
Dittany 1
Poppy ¼

Willow 1
Frankincense ¼
QB 1¾

Psychic #1

Safflower 3/4
Wormwood 1/4
Cinnamon 1/2

Dittany 1
Red Sandalwood 1/2
QB 11/2

Psychic #2

Cloves 1/4
Myrrh 1/4
Sandalwood 1

Dittany 3/4
Cinnamon 1/4
QB 11/2

Psychic Protection #1

Elder 1/2
Cinquefoil 1
FW 11/2

Bay 1/2
Valerian 1/8

Psychic Protection #2

Broom 1/4
Agrimony 1/2
Basil 1/2
LF 11/2

Cranesbill 1/4
Vetiver 1
Oregano 1/2

Psychic Protection #3

Angelica 1/2   Cloves 1/4
Galangal 1/2   Base 1/2
Red Clover 1 1/2   LF 1 3/4

Psychic Protection #4 (Loose only)

Dittany 1   Mistletoe 1/2
Cinquefoil 1   Frankincense 1/2

Psychic Protection #5

Dittany 1   St. Johnswort 1
Dragon's Blood 1/2   Wormwood 1/2
QB 1 1/2

Psychic Protection #6

Pine 1   Cassia 1/2
Sage 3/4   Mugwort 1/2
Spikenard 1/2   Water 1 3/4

Psychic Protection #7

Benzoin $1/2$
Frankincense $1/2$
Camphor $1/4$
Cassia $1/2$

Dragon's Blood $1/4$
Patchouli $1/4$
Sandalwood 2
QB $1^3/4$

Psychic Protection #8 (Loose only)

Mistletoe $1/4$
Patchouli $1/4$
Rue $1/4$
Dittany 1

Hyssop $1/4$
Frankincense $1/2$
Red Clover $3/4$

Recall Past Lives #1[†]

Sandalwood 1
Cinnamon $1/2$
Myrrh $1/2$
FW $1^1/4$

Myrrh Oil
Cinnamon Oil
Cucumber Oil

Recall Past Lives #2

Sandalwood $1^1/2$
Water Lily $1/2$
Holly $1/2$

Frankincense $1/2$
Lilac Oil
FW $1^1/2$

Release & Endings #1

Bay 1/2

Melilot 3/4

Rosemary 1/2

Quassia 1

Spearmint Oil

Water 1 1/2

Release & Endings #2

Bay 1/2

Lemon Balm 1/2

Pennyroyal 1/2

Willow 1

Yarrow 1/4

Lemon Balm Oil

Peppermint Oil

QB 1 1/2

Renewal #1

Red Clover 1 1/2

Allspice 1/2

LF 1 1/2

Garlic 1/2

Dragon's Blood 1/4

Renewal #2

Ginseng 1/4

Gotu Kola 1/2

QB 1 1/2

Life Everlasting 1/2

Rosemary 1 1/2

Renewal #3

Sage 1   Hemlock 1
Oak 1   QB 1$^{1}/_{2}$

Renewal #4

Rosemary 1   Dragon's Blood $^{1}/_{2}$
Sage $^{1}/_{2}$ Hemlock 1
FW 1$^{1}/_{2}$

Renewal #5

Aloes $^{1}/_{4}$ Sandalwood 1
Eucalyptus $^{1}/_{4}$ Lemon Oil
Holly $^{1}/_{2}$ Eucalyptus Oil
Marigold 1$^{1}/_{2}$ FW 1$^{1}/_{2}$

Rest & Sleep #1

Poppy $^{1}/_{2}$ Willow 1$^{1}/_{4}$
Camomile 1$^{1}/_{4}$ FW 1$^{1}/_{2}$

Rest & Sleep #2

Catnip $1/2$
Dill $1/2$
Poppy $1/4$
QB $1^{1/2}$

Lemon Verbena 1
Motherswort $1/2$
Lemon Verbena Oil

Spell Breaking #1 (Loose only)

Myrrh $1/4$
Nettle $1/2$
Slippery Elm $3/4$

Cinquefoil $1/2$
Willow $3/4$

Spell Breaking #2

St. Johnswort $1^{1/2}$
Burdock $1/2$
QB $1^{1/2}$

Rue $1/4$
Cloves $1/2$

Spell Breaking #3

Patchouli $1/4$
Willow $3/4$
QB $1^{1/2}$

St. Johnswort $3/4$
Slippery Elm $3/4$

Spirit Communication (Loose only)

Frankincense 1/2

Bay 3/4

Elder 1/4

Wormwood 1/2

Willow 1

Wisteria Oil

Stop Gossip #1 (Loose only)

Cloves 3/4

Nettle 1/2

Slippery Elm 1

Red Clover 1/2

Stop Gossip #2 (Loose only)

Deer's Tongue 1/2

Orris 1/2

Red Clover 1

Garlic 1/2

Strength #1

Dragon's Blood 1/2

Musk Root 1/2

Vetiver 1 1/2

QB 2

Cinquefoil 1/2

Musk Oil

Ambergris Oil

Strength #2

Cinnamon 1/2
Dragon's Blood 1/4
Frankincense 1/4
Musk Root 1/2
QB 1 1/2

Patchouli 1/4
Vetiver 1
Yarrow 1/4
Musk Oil

Success #1

Basil 1/2
Bay 1/2
QB 1 1/4

Cedar 1
Oak 1/2

Success #2

Mistletoe 1/4
Marigold 1/2
Sunflower 1/2
Water 1 1/2

Onion 1/4
Sandalwood 1
Bergamot Oil

Success #3

Solomon's Seal 1/2
Cedar 1 1/2
FW 1 1/4

Musk Root 1/2
Myrrh 1/4

Success #4

Frankincense 1/4
Vetiver 11/2
Angelica 1/4

Woodruff 1/2
Sandalwood 1
LF 13/4

Success #5

Bay 1/2
Frankincense 1/4
Mistletoe 1/2

Sandalwood 1
Cedar 3/4
FW 11/2

Success #6*

Sandalwood 11/2
Sarsaparilla 1/2
Motherwort 1/2

Quassia 1/2
Jasmine Oil
Water 13/4

Tranquility #1

Sage 1
Rose 11/2
Benzoin 1/4
LF 13/4

Meadowsweet 1/2
Base 1/2
Rose Oil

Tranquility #2

Cascarilla 1
Basil 1/4
Oregano 1/2
FW 1 1/2

Pennyroyal 1/2
Bay 1/2
Patchouli 1/4

Tranquility #3

Basil 1/2
Pennyroyal 1 1/4
Valerian 1/8
FW 1 1/4

Meadowsweet 1/2
Benzoin 1/2
Lilac Oil

Transformation #1 (Loose only)

Pennyroyal 1 1/2
Elder 1/4
Frankincense 1/2

Bay 1/2
Rosemary 1/2
Peppermint Oil

Transformation #2

Pomegranate 1
Slippery Elm 1 1/2
QB 1 1/2

Wormwood 1/2
Violet Oil

Transformation #3

Willow 1¼
Woodruff ½
QB 2

Ground Ivy ¾
Myrrh ½

Transformation #4

Holly ½
Pomegranate ½
Willow 1
FW 1¾

Frankincense ¼
Slippery Elm ½
Pennyroyal ½

Virility

Holly ½
Patchouli ¼
Savory ½
Mandrake ½
Civit Oil

Dragon's Blood ¼
Oak ½
Musk Root ¼
Musk Oil
FW 1½

Weather #1

Broom 1
Black Haw ½
QB 1½

Dragon's Blood ¼
Willow 1

Weather #2*

Benzoin 1½   Pinch of Salt
Dittany ½   Benzoin Oil
Black Haw ½   QB 1¼

RITUAL INCENSE

Ritual incense is any incense that is used for religious purposes. It is akin to magic, yet more subtle, since it is of a spiritual rather than material nature. It is used primarily to celebrate religious holidays and special spiritual or mystical happenings.

Although many of the recipes may seem to be esoteric in scope, they can still be used and enjoyed solely for their fragrances. The recipes included here are just a brief sampling of a virtually limitless number of ritual blends. Keep in mind that these recipes are geared to be measured in teaspoons (or fractions thereof). If you want to increase or decrease the quantities, see table of correspondences in Appendix 2 and 3 on pages 245 and 249. If you can't remember the recipes for the various bonding agents (QB, FW, or LF) see page 14.

Baby Blessing (Loose only)

Cinnamon ½	Sage ½
Frankincense ½	Cedar ½
Myrrh ¼	Patchouli ¼
Rose 1	Allspice ¼
Dittany ½	Benzoin ¼
Cinquefoil ¼	

Beltane #1*

Rose 1
Frankincense 1/2
Musk Root 1/2
Cinnamon 1/2
FW 11/2

Benzoin 1/4
Sandalwood 1/2
Musk Oil
Rose Oil

Beltane #2*

Benzoin 3/4
Rose 1/2
Rosemary 1/2
LF 11/2

Cinnamon 1/2
Sandalwood 3/4
Lemon Verbena Oil

Church #1 (Loose only)

Frankincense 1
Myrrh 3/4

Benzoin 1/2
Sandalwood 3/4

Church #2

Benzoin 1/2
Cascarilla 1/2
Sandalwood 1
QB 13/4

Vetiver 1/4
Musk Root 1/2
Frankincense 1/4

Circle #1 (Loose only)

Frankincense 1/2
Willow 1
Cinnamon 1/2
Patchouli 1/4

Cascarilla 1/2
Copal 1/4
Jalap 1/4

Circle #2

Bay 1/2
Camphor 1/2
Lavender 1/2
Yarrow 1/2

Broom 1/2
Linden 1/2
Ground Ivy 1/2
Water 2

Circle #3

Rosemary 1/2
Reed 1/2
Marjoram 1/2
Thyme 1/2

Basil 1/2
Linden 1/2
Lovage 1/2
QB 1 3/4

Circle #4

St. Johnswort 1/2
Cucumber 1/2
Mandrake 1/2
Dittany 1/2

Galangal 1/2
Juniper 1/2
Spikenard 1/2
FW 2

Circle #5

Sandalwood 1
Frankincense 1/2
Myrrh 1/4
Cinnamon 1/4
FW 1 1/2

Patchouli 1/4
Vervain 1/4
Orris 1/4
Mistletoe 1/4

Circle #6

Myrrh 1/2
Marjoram 1/4
Elder 1/4
Dragon's Blood 1/2

Willow 1
Oak 1/2
Pine 3/4
LF 2

Circle #7

Bay 1/2
Oak Moss 1/2
Cinquefoil 1/2
Rose 1/2

Dragon's Blood 1/2
Juniper 1/2
Spikenard 1/2
FW 1 3/4

Circle #8 (Loose only)

Frankincense 1/2
Willow 1
Star Anise 1/2
Benzoin 1/2

Ginger 1/4
Cedar 1/2
Jalap 1/4

Circle #9

Frankincense 1/4
Willow 1
Cinquefoil 1/2
Dittany 1/2

Dragon's Blood 1/4
Oak 1/2
Solomon's Seal 1/4
QB 1 1/2

Circle #10 (Loose only)

Frankincense 1/2
Poppy 1/4
Pomegranate 1/2
Red Clover 1

Basil 1/4
Cedar 1/2
Cascara Sagrada 1/2

Consecration #1 (Loose only)

Frankincense 1
Myrrh 1/4
Storax 1/4

Benzoin 1/2
Sandalwood 1 1/2
Bay 1/2

Consecration #2

Rosemary 1
St. Johnswort 1
Solomon's Seal 1/2

Sage 1/2
Hyssop 1/4
QB 1 1/2

Consecration #3

Bay 1/2
Pine 1
Rose 1

Thyme 1/2
Lavender 1/2
QB 11/2

Consecration #4

Cedar 1
Cinnamon 1/2
Dragon's Blood 1/4

Sage 3/4
Lovage 1/2
QB 11/2

Consecration #5

Elder 1
Onion 1/4
Star Anise 1/2
LF 13/4

Thyme 1/2
Broom 1/2
Sandalwood 1

Consecration #6

Rosemary 1
Lavender 1
Frankincense 1/4
Basil 1/2

Vervain 1/4
Valerian 1/8
Sage 1/4
FW 11/2

East #1 — (Raphiel)* (Loose only)

Angelica 6
Frankincense 3/4
Myrrh 3/4
Copal 1/4

Mastic 1/4
Mugwort 12
Galangal Oil 11/2

East #2

Lavender 3/4
Benzoin 1/4
Cinnamon 1/2
QB 11/2

Rose 1
Cherry 1/2
Rose Oil

East #3

Oregano 1
Sandalwood 1/2
Thyme 1/2
Pennyroyal 1/2

Star Anise 1/2
Peppermint Oil or
Spearmint Oil
QB 11/2

Esbat #1

Sandalwood 1
Frankincense 1/2
Myrrh 1/4
Cinnamon 1/2
QB 13/4

Vervain 1/4
Dittany 1/2
Patchouli 1/4
Bay 1/2

Esbat #2

Patchouli 1/2
Calamus 1/4
Mugwort 1/4
Cinnamon 1/2
Water 13/4

Camphor 1/4
Sandalwood 1
Ambergris Oil or
Musk Oil

Exodus XXX 23–24

Myrrh 1/2
Cassia 3/4
LF 11/2

Calamus 1/4
Sandalwood 1

Exodus XXX 34 (Loose only)

Cinnamon 1/2
Cloves 1/4
Ginger 1/4
Storax 1/4

Spikenard 1/4
Benzoin 1/4
Frankincense 3/4
Sandalwood 11/2

Fall

Oak 1/4
Pine 1/2
Frankincense 1/4
Cinnamon 1/4
QB 11/2

Cloves 1/4
Rosemary 1/2
Sage 1/4
Pomegranate 1/2

Funeral #1

Marjoram $^1/_2$ Thyme $^3/_4$
Melilot $^3/_4$ Willow 1
QB $1^1/_2$

Funeral #2

Oregano $^3/_4$ Poppy $^1/_4$
Lily of the Valley $^1/_2$ Willow 1
Lemon Balm $^1/_2$ Lily of the Valley Oil
QB $1^1/_2$

Funeral #3

Myrrh $^1/_4$ Rue $^1/_4$
Yew $^1/_4$ Parsley $^1/_4$
Yarrow 1   Pine Oil
Pine 1   QB $1^1/_2$

Funeral #4*

Patchouli 1   Pine (bark) 1
Yew 1   Birch Oil
QB $1^3/_4$

Hallows #1

Frankincense $1/2$
Myrrh $1/4$
Bay $1/2$
Vervain $1/4$
QB $13/4$

Wormwood $1/4$
Patchouli $1/4$
Cinnamon $1/2$
Sandalwood $1/2$

Hallows #2

Dittany 1
Pine $1/2$
Sandalwood 1
QB $13/4$

Patchouli $1/4$
Benzoin $1/4$
Pine Oil

Hallows #3*

Benzoin $1/2$
Dittany $11/2$

Patchouli 1
LF $11/2$

Kyphi (Loose only)

Honey 3/4
3 Raisins
Copal 1/4
Myrrh 1/4
Reed 1/4
Orris 1/4
Sandalwood 1
Storax 1/4

Galangal 1/2
Juniper 1/2
Broom 1/4
Calamus 1/2
Frankincense 1/2
Benzoin 1/2
Cinnamon 1/2
Wine (enough to make mixture moist)

Allow to dry before storing.

Lady Day (Loose only)

Juniper 1/2
Broom 1/2
Rose 1

Red Sandalwood 1
Frankincense 1/2
Rose Oil

Lammas

Broom 1/4
Oregano 1/2
Cinnamon 1/2
QB 1 1/2

Meadowsweet 1/2
Frankincense 1/4
Sandalwood 1/2

Mid-Eastern High Altar

Dittany 1
Sandalwood 1
Frankincense 1/2

Myrrh 1/4
Bay 1/2
QB 1 1/2

Moon Goddess* (Loose only)

Benzoin 6
White Onion Skins 3
Allspice 1 1/2

Camphor 1 1/2
Poppy 1/2
Olive Oil 1 1/4

North #1 — (Uriel)* (Loose only)

Angelica 6
Frankincense 3/4
Myrrh 3/4
Copal 1/4

Mastic 1/4
Life Everlasting 12
Myrrh Oil 1 1/2

North #2

Allspice 1/2
Cascara Sagrada 1
Deer's Tongue 1/4
QB 1 1/2

Musk Root 1/2
Red Sandalwood 1/2
Musk Oil

North #3

Cinquefoil ¹/₂
Damiana ¹/₂
Dittany 1
QB 1¹/₂

Patchouli ¹/₂
Red Clover ¹/₂
Wintergreen Oil

Pentacle #1

Frankincense ¹/₂
Willow ¹/₂
Patchouli ¹/₂

Sandalwood ¹/₂
Mistletoe ¹/₂
QB 1¹/₂

Pentacle #2

St. Johnswort ¹/₂
Willow 1
Dittany ³/₄

Marjoram ¹/₄
Mistletoe ¹/₄
Water 1¹/₂

Pentacle #3 (Loose only)

Dragon's Blood ¹/₂
Aloe ¹/₄
Mandrake ¹/₄

Benzoin ¹/₂
Mistletoe ¹/₄
Sandalwood 1

Pentacle #4

Rosemary 1/2
Oak Moss 1/2
Sage 1/2

Thyme 1/2
Mistletoe 1/2
QB 1 1/2

Pentacle #5

Oak 1/2
Oak Moss 1/2
Yarrow 1/2

Lavender 1/2
Mistletoe 1/2
Water 1 1/2

Pentacle #6 (Loose only)

Frankincense 1/2
Willow 1
Patchouli 1/4

Benzoin 1/2
Mistletoe 1/2

Proverbs 7:17 (Loose only)

Myrrh 1/2
Aloes 1/2

Cinnamon 1/2
Sandalwood 1 1/2

Roman Catholic (Loose only)

Frankincense 2
Benzoin 1

Storax $1/2$
Sandalwood 2

South #1 — Michiel* (Loose only)

Angelica 6
Frankincense $3/4$
Myrrh $3/4$
Copal $1/4$

Mastic $1/4$
Saffron 12
Frankincense Oil $1^{1}/2$

South #2

Cedar 1
Cloves $1/2$
Dragon's Blood $1/4$
QB $1^{1}/2$

St. Johnswort $3/4$
Sunflower $3/4$
Orange Oil

South #3

Basil $1/4$
Bay $1/2$
Frankincense $1/4$
LF $1^{1}/2$

Broom $1/4$
Rosemary 1
Cascarilla $1/2$

Spring

Primrose ¹/₄
Cherry 1
Rose 1
Sandalwood ¹/₂

Lilac Oil
Rose Oil
Strawberry Oil
QB 1³/₄

Summer #1

St. Johnswort 1
Mistletoe ¹/₂

Lavender 1¹/₂
Water 1¹/₂

Summer #2*

Cedar 1
Juniper ¹/₂

Sandalwood 1
QB 1¹/₂

Summer #3

Mugwort ¹/₂
Vervain ¹/₂
St. Johnswort 1
QB 1¹/₂

Frankincense ¹/₂
Mistletoe ¹/₄
Bay ¹/₄

Summer #4

Rose $^1/_2$

Orris $^1/_2$

Rosemary $^1/_2$

LF $1^1/_2$

Oak Moss $^1/_2$

Base $^1/_2$

Lemon Verbena Oil

Sun God* (Loose only)

Frankincense 1

Benzoin 1

Cinnamon 1

Corriander $^1/_2$

Olive Oil

Thanks Offering for a Completed Project*
(Loose only)

Frankincense $^3/_4$

Myrrh $^3/_4$

Ginger $^1/_8$ Vervain Oil

Rose (Pink) $^3/_4$

Thyme $^1/_8$

Cinquefoil $1^1/_2$

Wedding — Bridal Bower (Loose only)

Frankincense $1/2$	Linden $1/4$
Rose 1	Myrtle $1/4$
Sage $1/2$	Broom $1/4$
Rosemary $1/2$	Benzoin $1/4$
Lavender $1/2$	Sandalwood $1/2$
Jasmine Oil	Rose Oil

Wedding

Rose 1	Yarrow $1/2$
Marjoram $3/4$	Myrtle $1/4$
Linden $1/2$	Sandalwood $3/4$
Orange Oil	Rose Oil
Bayberry Oil	LF $1^{1}/2$

West — Gabriel* (Loose only)

Angelica 6	Mastic $1/4$
Frankincense $3/4$	Lemon Balm 12
Myrrh $3/4$	Storax $1/2$
Copal $1/4$	Ambergris Oil $1^{1}/2$

West

Willow 1½
Oak Moss ½
Poppy ¼
Camphor ¼

Cucumber ¼
Reed ¼
Jasmine Oil
QB 1½

Winter #1

Lavender 1¼
Cloves ½
Cinnamon ½
Orris ¼
QB 1¾

Benzoin ¼
Patchouli ¼
Mistletoe ¼
Bergamot Oil

Winter #2

Mistletoe ½
Holly ¼
Bay ½
Pine Oil
QB 1½

Oak ½
Pine 1
Cedar ½
Cedar Oil

Winter #3* (Loose only)

Copal ½
Frankincense 1
Myrrh ½

Pine 2
Oak ½

PLANETARY INCENSE

Each planet is thought to control certain aspects of life. For centuries, magic and the planets have been virtually inseparable. During the Middle Ages, the study of the planets and their magical spheres of influence was considered a science. Since then, countless books and articles have been written about the planets and their powers.

It is not within the scope of this book to give a detailed account of the planets and their various magical applications. Here are just a few examples of the various kinds of incense that are appropriate for each planet. These recipes may be used either in conjunction with planetary workings or burned solely for their fragrances.

All measurements for these recipes are in teaspoons (or fractions thereof). If you want to increase or decrease a recipe, see Appendix 2 and 3 (on pages 245 and 249) for conversion tables. If you cannot remember the recipe for the bonding agents used (QB, LF, and FW) turn back to page 14.

Sun #1

Bay 1	Orange 1
Angelica $1/2$	Base $3/4$
Mistletoe $1/4$	Orange Oil
LF $1^3/4$	

Sun #2 (Loose only)

Frankincense ¹/₂   Sunflower ¹/₂
St. Johnswort 1¹/₄   Orange ¹/₂
Marigold ¹/₄   Bergamot Oil

Sun #3

Rosemary 1¹/₄   Base ³/₄
Acacia ³/₄   Lemon Oil
Camomile ³/₄   LF 1¹/₄

Sun #4 (Loose only)

Frankincense ¹/₂   Rosemary 1
Safflower ¹/₂   St. Johnswort ¹/₂
Sunflower ¹/₂

Moon #1

Camphor ¹/₄   Aloe ¹/₄
Willow 1¹/₂   White Rose Oil or
Reed 1   Jasmine Oil
Water 1³/₄

Moon #2

Willow 1
Reed 1/2
Cucumber 1/4
Water 13/4

Water lily 1/2
Jasmine 1/2
Jasmine Oil or
Lotus Oil

Mercury #1

Lavender 11/2
Star Anise 1
Grains of Paradise 1/2

Bayberry 1/4
Bayberry Oil
QB 11/2

Mercury #2

Lavender 11/2
Cinnamon 3/4

Marjoram 1/2
Water 11/2

Mercury #3

Marjoram 11/2
Cinnamon 3/4
Wintergreen 1/2

Valerian 1/4
Wintergreen Oil
FW 11/2

Venus #1

Rose $1^{1}/_{2}$
Red Sandalwood 1
QB $1^{1}/_{2}$

Benzoin $^{1}/_{2}$
Rose Oil

Venus #2

Deer's Tongue $^{3}/_{4}$
Vetiver $1^{1}/_{4}$
Musk Root $^{1}/_{2}$
Water $1^{1}/_{2}$

Patchouli $^{1}/_{2}$
Ambergris Oil or
Musk Oil

Venus #3

Dittany $1^{1}/_{4}$
Pennyroyal 1
QB $1^{1}/_{4}$

Damiana $^{3}/_{4}$
Peppermint Oil

Venus #4

Red Clover 1
Thyme $^{3}/_{4}$
Sage $^{1}/_{2}$

Yarrow $^{1}/_{2}$
Civit Oil
QB $1^{1}/_{4}$

Venus #5

Red Sandalwood 1¼
Allspice ½
Orris ½
QB 1½

Musk Root ¼
Althea ¼
Musk Oil

Mars #1

Dragon's Blood ½
Broom ½
Cranesbill ¼

Sarsaparilla ½
Cascarilla ¾
LF 1½

Mars #2

Rue 1
Holly 1
QB 1¼

Tarragon ½
Ginger ¼

Mars #3

Dragon's Blood ½
Rue ¼
Wormwood ½

Turmeric ¼
Cascarilla 1
LF 1¼

Jupiter #1 (Loose only)

Oak $1^1/_2$

Juniper $^1/_2$

Cedar 1

Copal $^1/_4$

Pine $1^1/_2$

Jupiter #2

Lemon Balm 1

Linden $1^1/_2$

QB $1^1/_2$

Meadowsweet $^1/_2$

Lilac Oil

Jupiter #3

Balm of Gilead $^1/_4$

Oak 1

Hyssop $^1/_2$

Nutmeg $^1/_2$

Linden $^1/_2$

FW $1^1/_4$

Saturn #1

Ground Ivy 1

Cascara Sagrada $^3/_4$

Comfrey $^1/_4$

LF $1^1/_2$

Eucalyptus $^1/_4$

Quassia $^3/_4$

Eucalyptus Oil

Saturn #2

Scammony 1¼   Jalap ¼
Quassia 1½   Water 2

Saturn #3 (Loose only)

Hemlock 1½   Pine 1
Yew ½   Parsley ¼

KUN'S KITCHEN: GENERIC BLENDS

For those of you who don't have the time, space, need, or money to build up a large selection of herbs, you can make generic blends. These recipes contain ingredients which, for the most part, can be found in almost any spice rack or kitchen. The recipes are just as effective and pleasing as recipes with more exotic ingredients. Remember that the unit of measure for all these recipes is the teaspoon (or fraction thereof). If you wish to increase or decrease recipes, please see Appendices 2 and 3 on pages 245 and 249. If you can't remember how to make the bonding agent (QB, LF, or FW) please refer to page 14.

Animals

Oregano 1
Savory 1/2
Marjoram 1/4

Tarragon 1/4
Sandalwood 1
QB 1 1/2

Compassion

Allspice 1
Thyme 1

Sandalwood 1
Water 1 3/4

Confidence

Rosemary $3/4$ Garlic $1/4$
Thyme $1/2$ Tarragon $1/4$
Fennel $1/4$ Sandalwood $1/2$
Water $11/2$

Confidence & Determination

Rosemary 1   Garlic $1/4$
Thyme $11/4$ Allspice $1/4$
QB $11/4$

Consecration #1

Frankincense $1/2$ Sage $1/2$
Rosemary $3/4$ Cinnamon $1/2$
Bay $1/2$ Sandalwood $1/2$
LF $11/2$

Consecration #2

Frankincense $1/4$ Bay $1/2$
Sandalwood $3/4$ Cinnamon $1/2$
Thyme $1/4$ Star Anise $1/2$
Lovage $1/4$ QB $11/2$

Contact Other Planes

Frankincense $1/4$
Parsley $1/4$
Sandalwood $1^1/4$

Star Anise $1/2$
Thyme $1/2$
QB $1^1/2$

Determination

Allspice 1
Dill $1/2$

Sandalwood 1
QB $1^1/2$

Divination

Bay $1/2$
Frankincense $1/4$
Cloves $1/2$
QB $1^1/2$

Garlic $1/4$
Sage $1/2$
Sandalwood $3/4$

Divination & Spirit Communication

Sandalwood 1
Bay $1/2$
Frankincense $1/4$
Cinnamon $1/2$
QB $1^3/4$

Cloves $1/4$
Lovage $1/4$
Star Anise $1/4$
Thyme $1/4$

Divine Intervention

Bay 1
Frankincense 1/4

Sandalwood 1 1/2
QB 1 1/2

Dreams & Sleep

Frankincense 1/4
Star Anise 1/2
Sandalwood 1 1/2

Thyme 1/2
Nutmeg 1/4
Water 1 3/4

East

Star Anise 1/4
Cinnamon 1/2
Oregano 1/2

Sandalwood 1
Thyme 1/4
Water 1 1/2

End Negativity

Marjoram 1
Thyme 1
Oregano 1/2
Cloves 1/4

Bay 1/4
Allspice 1/4
Base 1/4
FW 1 1/2

End Nightmares

Star Anise $^1/_2$
Nutmeg $^1/_2$
QB 2

Dill $^1/_2$
Sandalwood $1^1/_2$

Exorcism #1 (Loose only)

Basil $^1/_2$
Bay $^1/_2$
Frankincense $^1/_2$
Garlic $^1/_4$

Onion $^1/_4$
Rosemary $^1/_2$
Sandalwood $^1/_2$

Exorcism #2

Frankincense $^1/_4$
Cloves $^1/_2$
Bay $^1/_2$

Garlic $^1/_4$
Sandalwood 1
QB $1^1/_2$

Fertility

Allspice $^3/_4$
Fennel $^1/_2$
QB $1^1/_2$

Star Anise $^3/_4$
Sandalwood 1

Fertility & Growth

Allspice $1/2$
Star Anise $1/2$
Mace $1/4$
QB $1 1/2$

Nutmeg $1/4$
Basil $1/2$
Thyme $1/2$

Gain

Allspice $3/4$
Coriander $1/4$
Fennel $1/4$

Star Anise $3/4$
Sandalwood $3/4$
QB $1 1/2$

Good Luck

Rosemary 1
Sandalwood 1
Water $1 3/4$

Star Anise $1/2$
Nutmeg $1/2$

Good Luck

Star Anise $1/2$
Rosemary $1/2$
Bay $1/2$

Frankincense $1/4$
Sandalwood 1
QB $1 1/2$

Good Luck & Success

Frankincense $1/4$
Sandalwood 1
Cinnamon $1/2$
Basil $1/4$

Sage $1/4$
Bay $1/4$
Rosemary $1/4$
FW $1^{1/2}$

Happiness

Marjoram $3/4$
Rosemary $3/4$
LF $1^{1/2}$

Oregano $3/4$
Sandalwood $3/4$

Herbal Garden

Lovage $1/2$
Oregano 1
Rosemary $1/2$
Sage $1/4$

Thyme $1/4$
Basil $1/4$
Bay $1/4$
QB $1^{1/2}$

Jupiter

Nutmeg $1/2$
Mace $1/4$

Sandalwood $1^{1/2}$
QB $1^{1/4}$

Keep Secret

Sage $3/4$
Caraway $1/4$
Dill $1/4$
QB $1^1/_2$

Coriander $1/2$
Tarragon $1/4$
Sandalwood 1

Knowledge & Wisdom

Rosemary $3/4$
Sage $3/4$
Cinnamon $1/2$

Cloves $1/2$
Bay $1/2$
QB $1^1/_2$

Love #1

Cloves $1/2$
Cinnamon $1/2$
Sage $1/4$
Lovage $1/4$
QB $1^1/_2$

Savory $1/4$
Oregano $1/2$
Bay $1/4$
Allspice $1/4$

Love #2

Rosemary $1/2$
Fennel $1/2$
Cinnamon $1/2$
QB $1^3/_4$

Oregano $1/2$
Cloves $1/2$
Sandalwood $1/2$

Magic

Cinnamon $1/2$	Sage $1/2$
Frankincense $1/4$	Thyme $1/2$
Bay $1/2$	Sandalwood $1/2$
Garlic $1/4$	QB $1^{1}/2$

Mars

Basil $1/2$	Tarragon $1/4$
Coriander $1/4$	Sandalwood 1
Onion $1/4$	QB $1^{1}/4$

Material Objects

Basil $1/2$	Sage 1
Cinnamon $3/4$	Sandalwood $3/4$
QB $1^{1}/2$	

Meditation #1

Parsley $1/2$	Rosemary 1
Sage 1	Thyme 1
LF $1^{3}/4$	

Meditation #2

Frankincense 1/4
Bay 1
Cinnamon 1/2

Nutmeg 1/2
Sandalwood 1/2
LF 1 1/2

Meditation #3

Frankincense 1/4
Sage 1/2
Rosemary 1

Cinnamon 1/2
Sandalwood 1/2
QB 1 1/2

Memory

Bay 1/2
Caraway 1/4
Cloves 1/2

Rosemary 3/4
Sandalwood 3/4
QB 1 1/2

Mercury

Star Anise 1/2
Cinnamon 1/2
Water 1 1/2

Sage 1/2
Sandalwood 1

Money #1

Basil 1
Cinnamon 1
Bay $1/2$
FW $1^1/2$

Lovage $1/4$
Garlic $1/4$
Nutmeg $1/4$

Money #2

Star Anise $3/4$
Thyme $1/2$
Garlic $1/4$

Bar $1/2$
Cinnamon $1/2$
QB $1^1/2$

North

Allspice $3/4$
Lovage $1/2$
Dill $1/4$

Sage $1/2$
Sandalwood $3/4$
QB $1^1/2$

Peace & Tranquility #1

Basil $1/4$
Thyme $1/2$
Sage $1/2$
Frankincense $1/4$

Bay $1/2$
Cinnamon $1/2$
Sandalwood $1/2$
LF $1^1/2$

Peace & Tranquility #2

Oregano 1/2

Cinnamon 1/2

Bay 1/2

QB 1 3/4

Frankincense 1/4

Sage 1/2

Sandalwood 1

Prevent Theft

Caraway 1/2

Rosemary 1 1/2

QB 1 1/2

Tarragon 1/4

Sandalwood 1/2

Protection #1

Frankincense 1/4

Sage 1/2

Star Anise 1/2

Tarragon 1/4

Sandalwood 1

QB 1 1/4

Protection #2

Basil 1/4

Cinnamon 1/2

Lovage 1/4

QB 1 1/2

Rosemary 1/2

Thyme 1/2

Sandalwood 3/4

Protection #3

Bay $^1/_2$
Cloves $^1/_2$
Garlic $^1/_4$

Oregano $^3/_4$
Sandalwood $^3/_4$
QB $1^1/_2$

Protection #4

Cloves $^1/_2$
Sandalwood $^1/_2$

Rosemary 2
FW $1^1/_2$

Psychic Protection

Frankincense $^1/_4$
Bay $^1/_2$
Cloves $^1/_2$
Ginger $^1/_4$
FW $1^1/_2$

Oregano $^1/_2$
Lovage $^1/_4$
Star Anise $^1/_4$
Sandalwood $^1/_2$

Rest & Sleep

Dill $^1/_2$
Nutmeg $^3/_4$

Sandalwood $1^1/_2$
QB $1^1/_2$

Saturn

Celery $1/4$
Parsley $1/4$
QB $1^{1}/4$

Dill $1/2$
Sandalwood 1

South

Basil $1/4$
Bay $1/2$
Cloves $1/2$
QB $1^{1}/2$

Frankincense $1/4$
Rosemary $3/4$
Sandalwood $1/2$

Stop Gossip

Cloves 1
Garlic $1/2$
QB $1^{1}/2$

Onion $1/4$
Sandalwood 1

Success

Basil $1/4$
Frankincense $1/4$
Garlic $1/4$

Bay $1/4$
Sandalwood $1^{1}/2$
QB $1^{1}/2$

Sun

Bay $1/2$
Cloves $1/4$
Frankincense $1/4$

Rosemary $1/2$
Sandalwood 1
QB $11/4$

Transformation

Bay $3/4$
Frankincense $1/4$
QB $11/2$

Rosemary 1
Sandalwood 1

Venus

Allspice $1/4$
Oregano $3/4$
Grains of Paradise $1/4$

Thyme $1/2$
Sandalwood 1
QB $11/2$

Appendix 1

Appendix I

COMMON NAMES OF HERBS & PLANTS

The following list contains some of the common or popular names of herbs listed in the herbal section of this book.

Absinthe . . . . .Wormwood
Acoron . . . . .Calamus
Adder's Mouth . . . .Chickweed
African Ju Ju Powder. .Galangal
Alabahaca . . . . .Basil
Alcanna . . . . .Henna
All-Heal . . . . .Mistletoe
                            Valerian
Alraun . . . . .Mandrake
Alum Root . . . . . . .Cranesbill
Amantilla . . . . .Valerian
Amaracus . . . . .Marjoram
Amber . . . . .St. Johnswort
                            Storax
American Acacia . . . . . .Locust
American Dittany . . . . . . .Basil
American Liquid
    Amber . . . . .Sweet Gum
American Saffron . . .Safflower
American Spikenard. .Spikenard
Anethum . . . . .Dill
Aniseed . . . . .Anise
Antew . . . . .Myrrh
Appleringie . . . .Southernwood
Archangel . . . . .Angelica

Argue Tree . . . . .Sassafras
Arovous . . . . .Willow
Artemisia . . . . .Mugwort
                            Wormwood
Asarum . . . . .Lavender
Asphaltus. . . . . .Broom
Baaras . . . . .Mandrake
Badiana . . . . .Star Anise
Balm . . . . .Lemon Balm
Balm Mint . . . .Balm of Gilead
Bamba Wood . . . . . . .Bamboo
Bamboo Briar . . . .Sarsaparilla
Banal . . . . .Broom
Banda Fruit . . . . .Mace
Bardana . . . . .Burdock
Basswood . . . . .Linden
Bat Tree . . . . .Elder
Bealadh . . . . .Broom
Bean Herb. . . . . .Savory
Bearberry . . . . .Uva Ursi
Bearsweed . . . . . . .Yerba Santa
Bee Balm . . . . .Bergamot
                            Lemon Balm
Begger's Buttons . . . . .Burdock
Begger's Crocus. . . . .Safflower

Benjamin. . . . . .Benzoin
Besom . . . . .Broom
Betony . . . . .Wood Betony
Birdlime . . . . .Mistletoe
Bishopwort . . . . .Wood Betony
Bitter Aloes . . . . .Aloes
Bitter Ash . . . . .Quassia
Bitter Mint. . . . . .Thyme
Bitter Wood . . . . .Quassia
Black Aphrodite . . . . .Yohimbe
Blessed Herb . . . . .Valerian
Bloodwort . . . . .Yarrow
Blue Gum . . . . .Eucalyptus
Blue Vervain. . . . . .Vervain
Blume. . . . . . . .Dragon's Blood
Boneset. . . . . .Comfrey
Bowl. . . . . .Myrrh
Boxberry . . . . .Wintergreen
Boxwood . . . . .Dogwood
Bramble Vine. . . . .Sarsaparilla
Brandy Mint. . . . . .Peppermint
Bridewort . . . . . .Meadowsweet
British Tobacco . . . . .Coltsfoot
Bruisewort. . . . . .Comfrey
Buckthorn . . .Cascara Sagrada
Bull's Blood. . . . . . .Horehound
Butterbur . . . . .Coltsfoot
Butter Rose . . . . .Primrose
Calabach. . . . . .Nutmeg
Calendula . . . . .Marigold
Cane. . . . . .Reed
Canada Pitch Tree. . .Hemlock
Candleberry . . . . .Myrtle
Cankerwort . . . . . . .Dandelion
Cape Aloes . . . . .Aloe
Cape Gum . . . . .Acacia
Capon's Tail. . . . . .Valerian
Cardamon. .Grains of Paradise
Carpenter's Weed . . . . .Yarrow

Carrageen . . . . .Irish Moss
Carrizo. . . . . .Reed
Casper's Flower. . . . . .Wisteria
Catarrh Root . . . . . . .Galangal
Catmint . . . . .Catnip
Cat's Foot . . . .Life Everlasting
Cat's Paw . . . . .Ground Ivy
Cedron . . . . . .Lemon Verbena
Chafeweed . . .Life Everlasting
Chameli. . . . . .Jasmine
Chamomile. . . . . . .Camomile
Checkerberry . . . .Wintergreen
Chewing John . . . . . .Galangal
Ch'iang. . . . . .Ginger
China Root. . . . . .Galangal
Chinese Anise . . . . . .Star Anise
Chinese Apple . . .Pomegranate
Chinese Cinnamon. . . . .Cassia
Chinese Parsley . . . .Coriander
Chinese Peppermint
   Oil. . . . . .Menthol
Chinwood . . . . .Yew
Chittem
   Bark . . . . . .Cascara Sagrada
Chocolate Flower . .Cranesbill
Chondrus . . . . .Irish Moss
Christ's Thorn . . . . .Holly
Church Steeples . . . .Agrimony
Cilantro. . . . . .Coriander
Cinnamon Wood . . . .Sassafras
Clear Eye. . . . . . . .Clary Sage
Cockleburr . . . . . . .Agrimony
                        Burdock
Compass Weed . . . . .Rosemary
Consolida. . . . . .Comfrey
Consumptive's
   Weed . . . . .Yerba Santa
Convallaria .Lily of the Valley
Copalm. . . . . .Sweet Gum

Cornel ....Dogwood
Corn Rose ....Poppy
Costus ....Calamus
Coughwort ....Coltsfoot
Cow Cabbage.....Water Lily
Creeping Jenny.....Bindweed
Crowfoot..........Cranesbill
Cuckoo's Bread ......Plantain
Cudweed.....Life Everlasting
Curcuma .... Turmeric
Daphne................Bay
Death Flower ....Yarrow
Death Plant ....Parsley
Deerberry ....Wintergreen
Devil's Dung ......Asafoetida
Devil's Eye ....Elder
Devil's Nettle.........Yarrow
Didin ....Myrrh
Dinkum ....Eucalyptus
Dittany of Crete......Dittany
Dog Daisy ....Yarrow
Dollof ....Meadowsweet
Donnhove ....Coltsfoot
Dragon Herb ....Tarragon
Drelip..............Primrose
Dropberry .....Solomon's Seal
Duck's Foot........Mandrake
Dwarf Palmetto.Saw Palmetto
Eglantine........Honeysuckle
Egyptian Paradise
    Seed.....Grains of Paradise
Egyptian Privet ....Henna
Egyptian Thorn ....Acacia
Elderberry.............Elder
Elf Dock ....Elecampane
Elf Leaf ....Lavender
Elfwort ....Elecampane
Ellhorn ....Elder
Elm...........Slippery Elm

Enchanter's Plant.....Vervain
English Cowslip .....Primrose
Estragon ....Tarragon
Evergreen ....Pine
Fairy Bells.......Wood Sorrel
Fairy Cups ....Primrose
False Acacia ....Locust
Fan Palm ......Saw Palmetto
Feathergrass............Reed
Felon Herb.........Mugwort
Fenkel ....Fennel
Ferula ....Asafoetida
                  Musk Root
Field Balm ....Catnip
Fieldhove ....Coltsfoot
Five-finger Fern ..Maidenhair
Five-finger Grass...Cinquefoil
Fleaseed ....Psyllium
Florentine Iris..........Orris
Food of the Gods...Asafoetida
Fox's Clote ....Burdock
Friar's Balsam ......Benzoin
Garclive..........Agrimony
Garden Balm....Lemon Balm
Garden Heliotrope ...Valerian
Garde-robe ....Southernwood
Gaulteria........Wintergreen
Gearwe..............Yarrow
Genevrier............Juniper
Genista ....Broom
Gillrun ....Ground Ivy
Gladdon............Calamus
Goat's Leaf ......Honeysuckle
Goat Weed .....St. Johnswort
Golden Bough ......Mistletoe
Golds.............Marigold
Gort ....Ground Ivy
Gravel Root ....Meadowsweet
Graveyard Dust.....Patchouli

Greek Mint . . . . .Dittany
Greek Nuts . . . . .Almond
Green Ginger. . . . .Wormwood
Green Incense . . . . .Cedar
Green Mint. . . . . . .Spearmint
Green Powder. . . . . .Musk
Green Spine . . . . . .Spearmint
Grenadier. . . . . . .Pomegranate
Ground Apple . . . . .Camomile
Guardrobe. . . . . . . .Rosemary
Guinea Pepper. . . . .Grains of
                    Paradise
Gum Arabic . . . . .Acacia
Gum Bush . . . . . . .Yerba Santa
Gum Plant. . . . . .Comfrey
Gum Thus . . . . .Frankincense
Gum Tree. . . . . . .Sweet Gum
Hachah . . . . .Acacia
Hadassim. . . . . .Myrtle
Han-Ch'in . . . . .Celery
Hardock . . . . .Burdock
Hart's Tongue . .Deer's Tongue
Hart's Tree . . . . .Melilot
Haw . . . . .Black Haw
Hay Flowers. . . . . .Melilot
Headache. . . . . .Poppy
Hedgemaids . . . . . .Ground Ivy
Herb Louisa . .Lemon Verbena
Herb of Circe . . . . .Mandrake
Herb of Grace. . . . . .Rue
                    Vervain
Herb of Kings . . . . .Basil
Herb of Repentence . . . . . .Rue
Herb Peter. . . . . .Primrose
Herb Walter . . . . . . .Woodruff
High John
    the Conqueror . . . . . . .Jalap
Hollunder . . . . .Elder

Holy Herb . . . . .Hyssop
    Vervain, Yerba Santa
Holy Tree . . . . .Holly
Honey Locust . . . . .Locust
Honey Plant. . . . .Lemon Balm
Horse Heal . . . . . .Elecampane
Horse Hoof . . . . .Coltsfoot
Hu .Oak
Hulm . . . . .Holly
Hypericum . . . . .St. Johnswort
Incensier . . . . .Rosemary
Indian Elm . . . . .Slippery Elm
Indian Root. . . . . . . .Spikenard
Inn-Sai . . . . .Parsley
Irish Daisy . . . . . . .Dandelion
Iris Root. . . . . .Orris
Ivy. . . . . .Ground Ivy
Jacob's Ladder. . . . .Lily of the
                    Valley
Jamaica Pepper . . . . . .Allspice
Japanese Isinglass . .Agar Agar
Jatamansi. . . . . . . .Musk Root
Juno's Tears. . . . . .Vervain
Kamai Melon . . . . . .Camomile
Karam . . . . .Myrrh
Khezama . . . . .Lavender
                    Marjoram
Khus Khus . . . . .Vetiver
King's Clover . . . . .Melilot
Klamathweed . . .St. Johnswort
Knitbone . . . . .Comfrey
Kuei . . . . .Juniper
Kummel . . . . .Caraway
Kyul . . . . .Orange
Lad's Love. . . . .Southernwood
Lady's Seal . . . .Solomon's Seal
Lamb's Mint. . . . . .Peppermint
                    Spearmint

Lammint.........Peppermint
Laos...............Galangal
Lappa..............Burdock
Laurel.................Bay
Lavose ....Lovage
Life of Man........Spikenard
Lime Tree ....Linden
Link................Broom
Lion's Ear ....Motherwort
Lion's Foot.....Lady's Mantle
Lion's Tooth.......Dandelion
Liquid Amber.........Storax
Little Dragon.......Tarragon
Loranthus ....Mistletoe
Love Flower............Rose
Love Leaves.........Burdock
Love Pods..Grains of Paradise
Love Root ....Orris
Low John ....Galangal
Luban..........Frankincense
Lucky Hand ....Salep
Macis ....Mace
Maiden's Ruin..Southernwood
Male Lily ...Lily of the Valley
Malicorio ....Pomegranate
Mandragora ....Mandrake
Man-root............Ginseng
Manzanilla ....Camomile
Marchalan ......Elecampane
Marigold of Peru ...Sunflower
Marrob ....Horehound
Marrubium ....Horehound
Marshmallow ....Althea
Master of the Wood .Woodruff
Masterwort ....Angelica
Mawseed ....Poppy
May Apple ....Mandrake
May Bells ...Lily of the Valley
May Lily ...Lily of the Valley

Maythen ....Camomile
Meadow Queen .Meadowsweet
Meadwort......Meadowsweet
Mecca Balsam .Balm of Gilead
Medudi ....Henna
Meeting House Seed ......Dill
Melissa ....Lemon Balm
Mexican Damiana ...Damiana
Mexican Frankincense ..Copal
Mignonette ....Henna
Milfoil...............Yarrow
Minari ....Celery
Molucca Spice.........Cloves
Monarda ....Bergamot
Mor..................Myrrh
Mortification Root.....Althea
Mosquito Plant....Pennyroyal
Mountain Balm...Yerba Santa
Mountain Mint .....Bergamot
                  Marjoram
Mountain Tea....Wintergreen
Moxa..............Mugwort
Muscatel Sage .....Clary Sage
Mu-Yao ....Myrrh
Nard ....Lavender
                  Spikenard
Nardus ....Lavender
Neroli...............Orange
Nila...................Lilac
Nine Hooks ....Lady's mantle
Nip ....Catnip
Norway Pine........Hemlock
Oak Scale ....Oakmoss
Oil of Cade ....Juniper
Old Man .....Southernwood
Old Man's Pepper.....Yarrow
Old Man's Root ....Spikenard
Old Woman......Wormwood
Olibanum.......Frankincense

Onycha . . . . .Spikenard
Opossum Tree . . . .Sweet Gum
Orchid Root . . . . .Salep
Orchis . . . . .Salep
Origanum . . . . .Oregano
Orvale . . . . .Clary Sage
Osier. . . . . .Willow
Oswego Tea. . . . . . . .Bergamot
Our Lady's Keys. . . . .Primrose
Our Lady's Mint . . .Spearmint
Our Lady's Tears. . .Lily of the
　　　　　　　　　　　　Valley
Oxalis. . . . . .Wood Sorrel
Pan Palm . . . . . .Saw Palmetto
Passerina . . . . .Chickweed
Passion Bark . . . . .Yohimbe
Password . . . . .Primrose
Pentaphyllon . . . . . .Cinquefoil
Pepper Grass. . . . .Pepperweed
Personata . . . . .Burdock
Pettymorell . . . . . . .Spikenard
Philanthropos . . . . . .Agrimony
Phu . . . . .Valerian
Pigeon Weed. . . . . .Spikenard
Piliolerial. . . . . . . .Pennyroyal
Pimento . . . . .Allspice
Pipe Tree. . . . . .Elder
Plume . . . . .Nutmeg
Polar Plant. . . . . . . .Rosemary
Poor Man's
　　Ginseng. . . . . . . .Gotu Kola
Poor Man's Treacle. . . . .Garlic
Poplar Buds . . .Balm of Gilead
Priest's Crown . . . . .Dandelion
Puchaput . . . . .Patchouli
Pudding Grass . . . .Pennyroyal
Purple Clover . . . . .Red Clover
Queen Elizabeth Root . . .Orris

Queen of the
　　Meadow . . . . .Meadowsweet
Red Berry . . . . .Ginseng
Red Sanders. .Red Sandlewood
Reseda . . . . .Henna
Ripple Grass . . . . . . .Plantain
Rock Fern. . . . . . Maidenhair
Rose Mallow . . . . .Hibiscus
Rubywood . . .Red Sandlewood
Ruddes . . . . .Marigold
Sabal . . . . .Saw Palmetto
Sacred Bark. .Cascara Sagrada
Sage of Bethlehem. .Spearmint
Saille. . . . . .Willow
Sailor's Tobacco. . . . .Mugwort
St. George's Herb . . . .Valerian
St. John's Plant . . . . .Mugwort
St. Josephswort . . . . .Basil
St. Mary's Seal .Solomon's Seal
Salsify. . . . . .Comfrey
Salvia. . . . . .Sage
Sambac . . . . .Jasmine
Sandarac . . . . .Cedar
Sanders. . . . . .Sandlewood
Sanguinary. . . . . .Yarrow
Santal . . . . .Sandlewood
Sappan . . . . . .Red Sandlewood
Satyrion . . . . .Salep
Satyr's Herb . . . . .Savory
Sawge . . . . .Sage
Saxifrax . . . . .Sassafras
Scabwort . . . . .Elecampane
Scarlet Monarda . . . .Bergamot
Sea Dew. . . . . .Rosemary
Sealwort . . . . . .Solomon's Seal
Sea Moss . . . . .Irish Moss
Seamsog. . . . . . . .Wood Sorrel
Sea Parsley. . . . . .Lovage
Sea Spirit. . . . . .Irish Moss

Sedge ....Calamus
Seed of Horus .....Horehound
Senna ....Cassia
Serah ....Lemon Grass
Setwell ....Valerian
Shakad..............Almond
Shoot of Paradise........Aloe
Slippery Root ....Comfrey
Snakeweed..........Plantain
Socotrine .....Dragon's Blood
Sourgrass........Wood Sorrel
Spiceberry.......Wintergreen
Spicebush ....Benzoin
Spignet............Spikenard
Spoonwood...........Linden
Squaw Mint .....Pennyroyal
Stacte ....Myrrh
Starwort..........Chickweed
Stellaria ......Lady's Mantle
Sterculia.............Karaya
Sticklewort ....Agrimony
Stinging Nettle........Nettle
Storkbill...........Cranesbill
Stracte ....Storax
Stringy Bark Tree..Eucalyptus
Styrax................Storax
Suan ....Garlic
Sumatra Gum ....Benzoin
Sumbul Root ......Musk Root
Summer's Bride .....Marigold
Sunkfield ....Cinquefoil
Sureau ....Elder
Sweet Balm .....Lemon Balm
Sweet Balsam .Life Everlasting
Sweet Bark ....Cascarilla
Sweet Clover ....Melilot
Sweet Flag..........Calamus
Sweet Lucerne.......Melilot
Sweet Sedge ....Calamus

Sweet Weed ....Althea
Sweet Wood ....Cassia
 Cinnamon
Swine's Snout......Dandelion
Synkefoyle ....Cinquefoil
Syrian Bindweed...Scammony
Syringia ....Lilac
Tae ....Bamboo
Tallow Shrub ....Myrtle
Tanner's Bark ....Oak
Tartar Root ....Ginseng
Tarweed........Yerba Santa
Teaberry ....Wintergreen
Thousand Leaf ....Yarrow
Throw Wort .....Motherwort
Tickweed.........Pennyroyal
Tilia ....Linden
Tinne.................Holly
Tore ....Jasmine
Tormentil ....Cranesbill
Tree of Doom..........Elder
Tree of Enchantment..Willow
Tree of Life ....Cedar
Trefoil ....Red Clover
Trumpet Weed..Meadowsweet
Ttalgi...........Strawberry
Tulsi ....Basil
Tungnamu ....Wisteria
Turnhoof ....Ground Ivy
Vandal Root.........Valerian
Vanilla leaf ....Deer's Tongue
Van Van ....Vervain
Velvet Dock......Elecampane
Venus' Hair.......Maidenhair
Venus' Tonic........Damiana
Verbena......Lemon Verbena
Verrucaria..........Marigold
Vetevert ....Vetiver
Victory Root ....Onion

Water Nymph . . . . . Water Lily
Waxberry . . . . Myrtle
Weeping Hemlock . . . Hemlock
Weeping Willow . . . . . . Willow
Wergulu . . . . Nettle
Weybroed . . . . Plantain
White Balsam . Life Everlasting
White Clover . . . . Clover
White Man's Foot . . . . Plantain
White
   Sandalwood . . . . Sandalwood
White Sanders . . . . Sandalwood
Wild Clover . . . . . . Red Clover
Wild Endive . . . . Dandelion
Wild Geranium . . . . Cranesbill
Wild Jalap . . . . Mandrake
                        Scammony
Wild Marjoram . . . . . . Oregano
Wild Strawberry . . Strawberry

Wild Sunflower . . Elecampane
Wild Vanilla . . . Deer's Tongue
Wintersweet . . . . Marjoram
Witch Herb . . . . Mugwort
Witches' Asprin . . . . . . Willow
Witches' Herb . . . . Basil
Woodbine . . . . Honeysuckle
Wood Musk . . . . Woodruff
Wood Shamrock . . Wood Sorrel
Woundwort . . . . Yarrow
Wycopy . . . . Linden
Wymote . . . . Althea
Yallac . . . . Comfrey
Yellow
   Sandalwood . . . . Sandalwood
Yu . . . . Slippery Elm
Yon . . . . Water Lily
Zanzibar Drop . Dragon's Blood
Zedoary . . . . Turmeric

Appendix 2

Appendix 2

INCREASING INCENSE RECIPES

Number of times increased				
1	2	3	4	5
1/8 tsp.	1/4 tsp.	3/8 tsp.	1/2 tsp.	5/8 tsp.
1/4 tsp.	1/2 tsp.	3/4 tsp.	1 tsp.	1 1/4 tsp.
1/2 tsp.	1 tsp.	1 1/2 tsp.	2 tsp.	2 1/2 tsp.
3/4 tsp.	1 1/2 tsp.	2 1/4 tsp.	1 Tbsp.	3 3/4 tsp.
1 tsp.	2 tsp.	1 Tbsp.	4 tsp.	5 tsp.
1 1/4 tsp.	2 1/2 tsp.	3 3/4 tsp.	5 tsp.	6 1/4 tsp.
1 1/2 tsp.	1 Tbsp.	4 1/2 tsp.	2 Tbsp.	7 1/2 tsp.
1 3/4 tsp.	3 1/2 tsp.	5 1/4 tsp.	7 tsp.	8 3/4 tsp.
2 tsp.	4 tsp.	2 Tbsp.	8 tsp.	10 tsp.
2 1/4 tsp.	4 1/2 tsp.	6 3/4 tsp.	3 Tbsp.	11 1/4 tsp.
2 1/2 tsp.	5 tsp.	7 1/2 tsp.	10 tsp.	12 1/2 tsp.
2 3/4 tsp.	5 1/2 tsp.	8 1/4 tsp.	11 tsp.	13 3/4 tsp.
1 Tbsp.	2 Tbsp.	3 Tbsp.	1/4 Cup	5 Tbsp.

INCREASING INCENSE RECIPES

Number of times increased			
6	8	10	12
³/₄ tsp.	1 tsp.	1¹/₄ tsp.	1¹/₂ tsp.
1¹/₂ tsp.	2 tsp.	2¹/₂ tsp.	1 Tbsp.
1 Tbsp.	4 tsp.	5 tsp.	2 Tbsp.
4¹/₂ tsp.	2 Tbsp.	7¹/₂ tsp.	3 Tbsp.
2 Tbsp.	8 tsp.	10 tsp.	¹/₄ Cup
7¹/₂ tsp.	10 tsp.	12¹/₂ tsp.	5 Tbsp.
3 Tbsp.	¹/₄ Cup	5 Tbsp.	6 Tbsp.
10¹/₂ tsp.	14 tsp.	17¹/₂ tsp.	7 Tbsp.
¹/₄ Cup	16 tsp.	20 tsp.	¹/₂ Cup
13¹/₂ tsp.	6 Tbsp.	22¹/₂ tsp.	9 Tbsp.
5 Tbsp.	20 tsp.	25 tsp.	10 Tbsp.
16¹/₂ tsp.	22 tsp.	27¹/₂ tsp.	11 Tbsp.
6 Tbsp.	¹/₂ Cup	10 Tbsp.	³/₄ Cup

Appendix 3

Appendix B

DECREASING INCENSE RECIPES

Fraction of Recipe			
1	3/4	2/3	1/2
4 Cups	3 Cups	2 2/3 Cup	2 Cups
3 Cups	2 1/2 Cups	2 Cups	1 1/2 Cups
2 1/2 Cups	30 Tbsp.	26 Tbsp. + 2 tsp.	1 1/4 Cups
2 Cups	1 1/2 Cups	1 1/3 Cup	1 Cup
1 3/4 Cup	21 Tbsp.	1 Cup + 8 tsp.	14 Tbsp.
1 1/2 Cups	18 Tbsp.	1 Cup	3/4 Cup
1 1/4 Cups	15 Tbsp.	3/4 Cup + 4 tsp.	10 Tbsp.
1 Cup	3/4 Cup	2/3 Cup	1/2 Cup
3/4 Cup	9 Tbsp.	1/2 Cup	6 Tbsp.
1/2 Cup	6 Tbsp.	16 tsp.	1/4 Cup
1/4 Cup	3 Tbsp.	8 tsp.	2 Tbsp.
3 Tbsp.	6 3/4 tsp.	6 tsp.	4 1/2 tsp.
2 Tbsp.	4 1/2 tsp.	4 tsp.	1 Tbsp.
1 Tbsp.	2 1/4 tsp.	2 tsp.	1 1/2 tsp.

DECREASING INCENSE RECIPES

Fraction of Recipe			
1/3	1/4	1/6	1/12
1 1/3 Cup	1 Cup	2/3 Cups	1/3 Cup
1 Cup	3/4 Cup	1/2 Cup	1/4 Cup
13 Tbsp. + 1 tsp.	10 Tbsp.	6 Tbsp. + 1 tsp.	10 tsp.
2/3 Cup	1/2 Cup	1/3 Cup	8 tsp.
1/2 Cup + 4 tsp.	7 Tbsp.	14 tsp.	7 tsp.
1/2 Cup	6 Tbsp.	1/4 Cup	2 Tbsp.
1/4 Cup + 8 tsp.	5 Tbsp.	10 tsp.	5 tsp.
1/3 Cup	1/4 Cup	8 tsp.	4 tsp.
1/4 Cup	3 Tbsp.	2 Tbsp.	1 Tbsp.
8 tsp.	2 Tbsp.	4 tsp.	2 tsp.
4 tsp.	1 Tbsp.	2 tsp.	1 tsp.
1 Tbsp.	2 1/4 tsp.	1 1/2 tsp.	3/4 tsp.
2 tsp.	1 1/2 tsp.	1 tsp.	1/2 tsp.

Appendix 4

Appendix

PLANETARY CORRESPONDENCE

Sun

Acacia	Frankincense	Myrrh
Angelica	Lemon	Orange
Bay	Lemon Grass	Rosemary
Bergamot	Locust	Safflower
Camomile	Marigold	St. Johnswort
Cloves	Mistletoe	Sunflower
Dandelion		

Moon

Agar Agar	Cucumber	Poppy
Bamboo	Hibiscus	Reed
Camphor	Irish Moss	Water Lily
Chickweed	Jasmine	Willow
Coconut	Oakmoss	

Mercury

Anise	Crabgrass	Sandalwood
Bayberry	Dill	Southernwood
Black Haw	Elecampane	Star Anise
Caraway	Fennel	Storax
Cassia	Lavender	Sweet Gum
Cinnamon	Mace	Tragacanth
Cinquefoil	Mandrake	Valerian
Clary Sage	Sage	Wintergreen

Venus

Allspice	Henna	Patchouli
Almond	Lady's Mantle	Pennyroyal
Althea	Lemon	Peppermint
Ambergris	Verbena	Pomegranate
Benzoin	Life	Primrose
Blueberry	Everlasting	Red Clover
Burdock	Lily of the	Red
Calamus	Valley	Sandalwood
Catnip	Lovage	Rose
Cherry	Maidenhair	Salep
Civit	Marjoram	Savory
Clover	Melilot	Saw Palmetto
Coltsfoot	Motherwort	Spearmint
Damiana	Mugwort	Strawberry
Deer's Tongue	Musk	Thyme
Dittany	Musk Root	Vervain
Dogwood	Myrtle	Vetiver
Elder	Orchid	Violet
Grains of	Oregano	Wisteria
Paradise	Orris	Yohimbe

Mars

Basil	Garlic	Onion
Broom	Ginger	Pepperweed
Cascarilla	Holly	Sarsaparilla
Coriander	Honeysuckle	Tarragon
Cranesbill	Menthol	Turmeric
Dragon's Blood	Mustard	Woodruff
Galangal	Nettle	Wormwood

Jupiter

Agrimony	Juniper	Nutmeg
Balm of Gilead	Lemon Balm	Oak
Cedar	Lilac	Plantain
Copal	Linden	Psyllium
Hyssop	Meadowsweet	Wood Betony

Saturn

Asafoetida	Ground Ivy	Scammony
Bindweed	Hemlock	Slippery Elm
Cascara	Horehound	Solomon's Seal
Sagrada	Jalap	Spikenard
Celery	Parsley	Spruce
Comfrey	Pine	Uva Ursi
Eucalyptus	Quassia	Yarrow
Ginseng	Rue	Yerba Santa
Gotu Kola	Sassafras	Yew

Appendix 5

ELEMENTAL CORRESPONDENCES

Air

Almond
Anise
Benzoin
Black Haw
Caraway
Cassia
Catnip
Cherry
Cinnamon
Dogwood
Elder
Fennel
Henna

Lavender
Lemon
  Verbena
Life
  Everlasting
Lily of the
  Valley
Mace
Marjoram
Mugwort
Orchid
Oregano

Pennyroyal
Peppermint
Primrose
Rose
Sandalwood
Savory
Spearmint
Star Anise
Thyme
Tragacanth
Violet
Wisteria

Fire

Acacia	Galangal	Nettle
Agrimony	Garlic	Nutmeg
Angelica	Ginger	Oak
Balm of	Holly	Onion
Gilead	Honeysuckle	Orange
Basil	Hyssop	Pepperweed
Bay	Juniper	Plantain
Bergamot	Lemon	Psyllium
Broom	Lemon Balm	Rose Geranium
Camomile	Lemon Grass	Rosemary
Cascarilla	Lilac	Safflower
Cedar	Linden	St. Johnswort
Cloves	Locust	Sarsaparilla
Copal	Marigold	Sunflower
Coriander	Meadowsweet	Tarragon
Cranesbill	Menthol	Turmeric
Dandelion	Mistletoe	Wood Betony
Dragon's	Mustard	Woodruff
Blood	Myrrh	Wormwood
Frankincense		

Water

See Moon in Appendix 4

Earth

Allspice
Althea
Ambergris
Asafoetida
Bayberry
Bindweed
Blueberry
Burdock
Calamus
Cascara
   Sagrada
Celery
Cinquefoil
Civit
Clary Sage
Clover
Coltsfoot
Comfrey
Crabgrass
Damiana
Deer's Tongue
Dill
Dittany
Elecampane
Eucalyptus
Gingseng

Gotu Kola
Grains of
   Paradise
Ground Ivy
Hemlock
Horehound
Jalap
Lady's
   Mantle
Lovage
Maidenhair
Mandrake
Melilot
Motherwort
Musk
Musk Root
Myrtle
Orris
Parsley
Patchouli
Pine
Pomegranate
Quassia
Red Clover
Red
   Sandalwood

Rue
Sage
Salep
Sassafras
Saw Palmetto
Scammony
Slippery Elm
Solomon's
   Seal
Southernwood
Spikenard
Spruce
Storax
Strawberry
Sweet Gum
Uva Ursi
Valerian
Vervain
Vetiver
Wintergreen
Wood Sorrel
Yarrow
Yerba Santa
Yew
Yohimbe

Appendix 6

Appendix o

MAGICAL USES OF HERBS

Animals

Protection of and from animals; calming and soothing of frightened or distraught animals; training or domesticating; attracting a familiar; creating a bond of love and trust, healing sick or injured animals.

Ambergris
Burdock
Catnip
Chickweed
Civit
Clover
Coltsfoot
Cranesbill
Dandelion
Deer's Tongue
Dogwood
Dragon's
    Blood
Elecampane
Ground Ivy
Honeysuckle
Horehound

Juniper
Lady's Mantle
Life
    Everlasting
Mandrake
Marjoram
Melilot
Mistletoe
Motherwort
Musk
Musk Root
Oregano
Peppermint
Pine
Plantain
Primrose
Red Clover

Reed
Rose
    Geranium
St. Johnswort
Savory
Southernwood
Spearmint
Spikenard
Tarragon
Uva Ursi
Valerian
Water Lily
Wintergreen
Wormwood
Yarrow
Yerba Santa

Aphrodisiac

Increase sexual drive and desire; enhance sensuality; overcome frigidity.

Almond	Gotu Kola	Pepperweed
Ambergris	Grains of	Rose
Anise	Paradise	Rose
Basil	Jasmine	Geranium
Bay	Juniper	Rosemary
Bergamot	Lavender	Sage
Calamus	Lovage	Salep
Caraway	Maidenhair	Sarsaparilla
Cassia	Mandrake	Savory
Celery	Mugwort	Saw Palmetto
Cinnamon	Musk	Southernwood
Civit	Musk Root	Spearmint
Cloves	Mustard	Star Anise
Coriander	Myrtle	Tarragon
Cranesbill	Nettle	Turmeric
Cucumber	Nutmeg	Valerian
Damiana	Onion	Vervain
Garlic	Orchid	Violet
Ginger	Parsley	Wormwood
Ginseng	Peppermint	Yohimbe

Beauty

Enhance natural and inner beauty; perceive beauty in all things.

Bay	Chickweed	Henna
Camomile	Coconut	Lady's Mantle
Celery	Elecampane	Lemon

(Beauty cont.)

Linden	Orchid	Strawberry
Maidenhair	Rose	Violet
Orange	Salep	Water Lily

Brighten Disposition and Happiness

Attracts joy and well-being; causes enjoyment and contentment; dispells sadness, bad moods, and irritability.

Basil	Lily of the	Myrtle
Dittany	Valley	Orange
Grains of	Marigold	Oregano
Paradise	Marjoram	Parsley
Jasmine	Melilot	Peppermint
Lemon Balm	Motherwort	Rosemary
Lemon	Myrrh	Spearmint
Verbena		

Clairvoyance and Divination

Attracts, enhances, and removes obstacles for better results; clarifies messages and signs.

Anise	Clary Sage	Hibiscus
Althea	Cloves	Holly
Basil	Coriander	Honeysuckle
Bay	Dittany	Lavender
Cassia	Elder	Lemon Grass
Cedar	Frankincense	Lilac
Cinnamon	Garlic	Marigold
Cinquefoil	Ground Ivy	Mugwort

(Clairvoyance and Divination cont.)

Nutmeg	Reed	Strawberry
Oak Moss	Rose	Sunflower
Onion	Safflower	Thyme
Parsley	Sage	Willow
Patchouli	Sandalwood	Wormwood
Pine	Southernwood	Yarrow
Poppy	Star Anise	Yew

Commanding

Enhances leadership abilities; aids in obtaining position of leadership or responsibility; strengthens will.

Ambergris	Melilot	Safflower
Basil	Menthol	St. Johnswort
Calamus	Musk	Slippery Elm
Catnip	Musk Root	Spikenard
Civit	Mustard	Storax
Elder	Oak	Sunflower
Fennel	Onion	Tarragon
Galangel	Orris	Turmeric
Garlic	Patchouli	Vetiver
Jalap	Pepperweed	Woodruff
Marigold	Poppy	Yohimbe

Compassion

Softens emotions; attracts aid and understanding; brings inner feelings to surface.

Allspice	Broom	Elder
Almond	Burdock	Lady's Mantle

(Compassion cont.)

Lemon Balm	Poppy	Sassafras
Motherwort	Primrose	Thyme
Myrrh	Quassia	Willow
Myrtle	Rose	Yew
Pine	Rue	

Confidence and Courage

Gives confidence; strengthens resolve; increases one's ability to cope with problems.

Cranesbill	Mustard	St. Johnswort
Fennel	Oak	Tarragon
Garlic	Rose	Thyme
Musk	Geranium	Turmeric
Musk Root	Rosemary	

Consecration

Purifies; psychic and spiritual cleansing; removes negative influences.

Anise	Cassia	Elder
Asafoetida	Cedar	Eucalyptus
Basil	Cinnamon	Frankincense
Bay	Clary Sage	Galangal
Broom	Copal	Garlic
Burdock	Cranesbill	Holly
Cascara	Dragon's	Hyssop
Sagrada	Blood	Jalap

(Consecration cont.)

Lavender	Rose	Star Anise
Lovage	Rose Geranium	Storax
Mistletoe	Rosemary	Thyme
Mugwort	Rue	Valerian
Musk	Sage	Vervain
Musk Root	Sandalwood	Willow
Myrrh	Scammony	Wood Betony
Onion	Solomon's Seal	Woodruff
Peppermint	Spearmint	Yarrow
Pine		

Contact Other Planes

Aids in all occult matters; enhances contact; helps recall past lives; receives messages from the dead.

Acacia	Galangal	Rose
Althea	Hibiscus	Sandalwood
Angelica	Holly	Southernwood
Anise	Hyssop	Star Anise
Black Haw	Lemon	Storax
Cascara	Lemon Grass	Thyme
Sagrada	Linden	Violet
Copal	Locust	Wintergreen
Damiana	Mistletoe	Wisteria
Dittany	Oak Moss	Wormwood
Elder	Parsley	Yarrow
Frankincense	Patchouli	

Determination

Increases will-power; enhances tenacity and perseverance; increases and strengthens determination.

Allspice	Dill	Psyllium
Althea	Hibiscus	Southernwood
Camomile	Honeysuckle	Willow
Crabgrass	Plantain	Wormwood

Dreams and Sleep

Prevents nightmares or negative dreams; attracts pleasant or insightful dreams; calms and relaxes; provides protection during sleep.

Camomile	Linden	Peppermint
Catnip	Marigold	Primrose
Dill	Motherwort	Poppy
Jasmine	Mugwort	Spearmint
Lemon	Nutmeg	Sunflower
Verbena		

Exorcism and Spell Breaking

Removes unwanted or malignant influences; casts out evil or negativity from a person, place, or thing; removes curses or spells; sends spells back to the sender.

Angelica	Bay	Burdock
Asafoetida	Benzoin	Cascara
Basil	Broom	Sagrada

(Exorcism and Spell Breaking cont.)

Cinquefoil	Myrrh	Slippery Elm
Cloves	Nettle	Solomon's Seal
Comfrey	Oak Moss	Southernwood
Copal	Onion	Storax
Cranesbill	Orris	Sweet Gum
Frankincense	Patchouli	Tumeric
Galangal	Pepperweed	Valerian
Garlic	Rose	Willow
Lemon	Geranium	Wormwood
Verbena	Safflower	Yarrow
Menthol	St. Johnswort	Yerba Santa
Mustard	Salep	

Fertility

Increases fertility of body, mind and spirit; causes the propagation of ideas or plans; increases productiveness and accomplishment.

Allspice	Grains of	Oak
Almond	Paradise	Orange
Anise	Hemlock	Pine
Basil	Jasmine	Plantain
Blueberry	Juniper	Pomegranate
Caraway	Karaya	Poppy
Celery	Mace	Psyllium
Cherry	Mandrake	Saw Palmetto
Coconut	Mistletoe	Spruce
Coriander	Motherwort	Star Anise
Cucumber	Mustard	Strawberry
Dill	Myrtle	Sunflower
Fennel	Nutmeg	Yarrow

Fidelity

Ensures good faith and loyalty; enhances integrity; insures performance of obligations or vows.

Basil	Ground Ivy	Psyllium
Caraway	Honeysuckle	Red
Dogwood	Horehound	Sandalwood
Dragon's	Lemon Grass	Rosemary
Blood	Plantain	Violet

Gain

Helps reach goals; aids in mental or spiritual growth; helps development of plans; insures prosperity and growth of material possessions.

Acacia	Coriander	Mistletoe
Agrimony	Cucumber	Mustard
Allspice	Dill	Nutmeg
Aloe	Fennel	Plantain
Angelica	Ginseng	Pomegranate
Anise	Gotu Kola	Poppy
Bamboo	Grains of	Psyllium
Blueberry	Paradise	Saw Palmetto
Caraway	Henna	Star Anise
Cedar	Juniper	Strawberry
Cherry	Karaya	Sunflower
Coconut	Mace	

Gentleness

Causes calmness and serenity; promotes a peaceful nature; stimulates moderation; blunts temper.

Camomile	Lily of the	Sassafras
Henna	Valley	Slippery Elm
Lady's Mantle	Maidenhair	Violet
Lavender	Meadowsweet	Willow
Lemon Balm	Motherwort	Wisteria
Lilac		

Good Luck

Causes gain or increase; attracts good fortune and prosperity; ends bad luck.

Anise	Honeysuckle	Rose
Agrimony	Irish Moss	Rosemary
Bay	Jalap	Rue
Bayberry	Lavender	St. Johnswort
Bindweed	Linden	Salep
Camomile	Mace	Sandalwood
Cascara	Marigold	Scammony
Sagrada	Meadowsweet	Spearmint
Cassia	Melilot	Solomon's Seal
Cinnamon	Mistletoe	Star Anise
Clover	Musk	Sunflower
Dandelion	Musk Root	Vetiver
Dragon's Blood	Myrrh	Violet
Frankincense	Nutmeg	Wintergreen
Galangal	Orange	Wood Sorrel
Grains of	Peppermint	Yarrow
Paradise	Red Clover	

Harmony

Promotes co-operation and accord; brings mutual agreement and understanding.

Acacia	Cinnamon	Meadowsweet
Althea	Clary Sage	Motherwort
Basil	Hibiscus	Oregano
Bay	Lavender	Pennyroyal
Bayberry	Lemon	Poppy
Benzoin	Verbena	Primrose
Calamus	Lilac	Rose
Camomile	Locust	Sage
Cassia	Maidenhair	Valerian
Catnip	Marjoram	Violet

Honesty

Promotes and protects honesty; reinforces trust and truthfulness; insures loyalty; protects from temptation.

Basil	Ground Ivy	Psyllium
Caraway	Honeysuckle	Red
Dogwood	Horehound	Sandalwood
Dragon's	Lemon Grass	Rosemary
Blood	Plantain	Violet

Increase the Power of Spells

Acacia	Frankincense	Musk Root
Ambergris	Galangal	Patchouli
Cassia	Lemon	St. Johnswort
Cinnamon	Lemon	Storax
Cinquefoil	Verbena	Sweet Gum
Civit	Locust	Vetiver
Copal	Menthol	Yarrow
Damiana	Musk	Yohimbe
Dragon's Blood		

Keep Secret

Protect ideas and information; conceal knowledge; make information incomprehensible or seem unimportant to others.

Agrimony	Ground Ivy	Oak
Caraway	Honeysuckle	Pomegranate
Clary Sage	Horehound	Rose
Coriander	Juniper	Sage
Crabgrass	Lavender	Sarsaparilla
Dill	Life	Tarragon
Dogwood	Everlasting	

Knowledge and Wisdom

Stimulates creativity and imagination; brings comprehension; increases perception and understanding; causes clear thinking; improves good judgment, intelligence, and common sense.

Angelica	Balm of Gilead	Bay

(Knowledge and Wisdom cont.)

Benzoin	Clary Sage	Solomon's Seal
Cassia	Honeysuckle	Vervain
Cinnamon	Rosemary	Wisteria
Cinquefoil	Sage	

Longevity

Increases life span of ideas, projects, groups, etc.; aids in perpetuation, endurance and continuation.

Cedar	Life	Rose
Fennel	Everlasting	Rosemary
Garlic	Mugwort	Rue
Ginseng	Myrtle	Sage
Gotu Kola	Oak	Yarrow
Lemon Balm	Primrose	

Love

Attracts those of like mind; strengthens love and affection; causes attachments and bonds to grow.

Allspice	Bay	Catnip
Almond	Benzoin	Celery
Ambergris	Bergamot	Cherry
Angelica	Bindweed	Cinnamon
Anise	Burdock	Cinquefoil
Balm of	Calamus	Civit
Gilead	Caraway	Clary Sage
Basil	Cassia	Cloves

(Love cont.)

Coriander	Mace	Rose
Cranesbill	Maidenhair	Rose Geranium
Cucumber	Mandrake	Rosemary
Damiana	Marigold	Rue
Deer's Tongue	Marjoram	Sage
Dill	Meadowsweet	Savory
Dragon's	Mistletoe	Saw Palmetto
Blood	Motherwort	Scammony
Elder	Musk	Southernwood
Elecampane	Musk Root	Spearmint
Fennel	Mustard	Spikenard
Galangal	Myrtle	Star Anise
Ginger	Nutmeg	Strawberry
Ginseng	Orange	Sunflower
Grains of	Orchid	Tarragon
Paradise	Oregano	Thyme
Honeysuckle	Orris	Valerian
Jalap	Patchouli	Vetiver
Jasmine	Pennyroyal	Vervain
Juniper	Peppermint	Violet
Lavender	Plantain	Willow
Lemon Balm	Poppy	Wisteria
Lemon	Primrose	Wood Sorrel
Verbena	Psyllium	Wormwood
Lilac	Quassia	Yarrow
Linden	Red	Yohimbe
Lovage	Sandalwood	

Magic

Helps all occult matters; aids in clairvoyance and divination; increases power of herbs; influences worldly events.

Angelica	Broom	Clover
Bay	Cinquefoil	Dandelion

(Magic cont.)

Dragon's Blood	Mugwort	Salep
Elder	Nettle	Slippery Elm
Elecampane	Oak	Southernwood
Frankincense	Oak Moss	Storax
Galangal	Onion	Thyme
Garlic	Patchouli	Turmeric
Holly	Pine	Valerian
Lavender	Primrose	Vervain
Lemon	Red Clover	Willow
Verbena	Rose	Woodruff
Mandrake	Rue	Wood Sorrel
Mistletoe	Safflower	Wormwood
Myrrh	St. Johnswort	Yarrow
Myrtle		

Material Objects

Helps to obtain, protect, attract, and increase possessions.

Agrimony	Clary Sage	Orange
Almond	Crabgrass	Peppermint
Basil	Honeysuckle	Pomegranate
Bayberry	Hyssop	Poppy
Bergamot	Jalap	Sage
Bindweed	Jasmine	Scammony
Camomile	Mandrake	Solomon's Seal
Cassia	Marigold	Spearmint
Cedar	Myrrh	Sunflower
Cinnamon	Myrtle	Vervain
Cinquefoil	Oak	

Meditation

Keeps out interference; increases concentration.

Acacia	Dittany	Parsley
Camomile	Frankincense	Rosemary
Cassia	Jasmine	Sage
Cinnamon	Locust	Sandalwood
Clary Sage	Nutmeg	Thyme
Copal		

Memory

Increases and strengthens memory; aids in recall.

Bay	Lavender	Patchouli
Benzoin	Life	Rose
Caraway	Everlasting	Rosemary
Cloves	Lilac	Yew
Honeysuckle	Marigold	

Modesty

Frees from excesses; promotes humility and reserve; protects purity and virtue; moderation.

Broom	Lilac	Maidenhair
Camomile	Lily of the	Reed
Lady's Mantle	Valley	Violet

Money and Wealth

Attracts and protects from loss; removal of debt; increase of resources, property, and material objects.

Acacia	Comfrey	Myrtle
Agrimony	Dragon's Blood	Nutmeg
Almond	Galangal	Orange
Anise	Garlic	Peppermint
Basil	Ginseng	Red Clover
Bay	Honeysuckle	Scammony
Bayberry	Hyssop	Salep
Bindweed	Irish Moss	Solomon's Seal
Camomile	Jalap	Spearmint
Cascara	Lavender	Spikenard
Sagrada	Locust	Star Anise
Cassia	Lovage	Sunflower
Cinnamon	Mandrake	Thyme
Cinquefoil	Marigold	Wintergreen
Clover	Meadowsweet	

Overcome Opposition

Removes obstacles to goal; helps to prevail; insures winning; surmounts difficulties.

Asafoetida	Jalap	Southernwood
Bay	Melilot	Valerian
Clover	Oak	Woodruff
Cloves	Onion	Wood Sorrel
Crabgrass	Red Clover	Wormwood
Garlic	St. Johnswort	

Passion

Physical love; causes desire and lust; increases emotion; stimulates enthusiasm.

Ambegris	Cranesbill	Rose
Basil	Ginger	Geranium
Broom	Jasmine	Savory
Caraway	Musk	Saw Palmetto
Cassia	Musk Root	Tarragon
Cinnamon	Mustard	Turmeric
Civit	Pepperweed	Yohimbe

Peace and Tranquility

Brings accord and agreement; aids in reconciliation; causes tranquility, serenity, and peace of mind; freedom from disturbance or interruption.

Acacia	Cinnamon	Marjoram
Althea	Clary Sage	Meadowsweet
Basil	Dill	Motherwort
Bay	Hibiscus	Oregano
Bayberry	Lavender	Pennyroyal
Benzoin	Lemon	Poppy
Calamus	Verbena	Primrose
Camomile	Lilac	Rose
Cascarilla	Linden	Sage
Cassia	Locust	Valerian
Catnip	Maidenhair	Violet

Prevent Theft

Guards objects; makes things hard to locate or steal.

Caraway	Horehound	Rosemary
Dogwood	Juniper	Tarragon
Ground Ivy	Mugwort	Willow
Honeysuckle		

Protection

Insures emotional and physical well-being; preserves from loss, injury, or annoyance; guards against evil or negativeness; attracts good luck.

Acacia	Cassia	Garlic
Agrimony	Cinnamon	Ground Ivy
Angelica	Cinquefoil	Hemlock
Anise	Clary Sage	Holly
Asafoetida	Clover	Horehound
Balm of	Cloves	Hyssop
Gilead	Comfrey	Irish Moss
Basil	Copal	Jalap
Bay	Cranesbill	Juniper
Benzoin	Dill	Lavender
Bergamot	Dogwood	Lemon
Bindweed	Dragon's	Verbena
Broom	Blood	Lily of the
Burdock	Elder	Valley
Caraway	Eucalyptus	Locust
Cascara	Fennel	Lovage
Sagrada	Frankincense	Mace

(Protection cont.)

Mandrake
Marigold
Marjoram
Mistletoe
Mugwort
Mustard
Myrrh
Nettle
Nutmeg
Oak
Onion
Oregano
Orris
Patchouli
Pennyroyal
Peppermint
Pine

Primrose
Quassia
Red Clover
Red
   Sandalwood
Rose
   Geranium
Rosemary
Rue
Sage
St. Johnswort
Sandalwood
Sarsaparilla
Scammony
Slippery Elm
Solomon's Seal
Spearmint

Spruce
Star Anise
Storax
Sunflower
Sweet Gum
Tarragon
Thyme
Uva Ursi
Vervain
Vetiver
Wisteria
Wood Betony
Woodruff
Wormwood
Yarrow
Yerba Santa
Yew

Psychic Development and Growth

Psychic development and growth is aided, protected, increased, and speeded towards fulfillment.

Acacia
Althea
Anise
Basil
Bay
Camphor
Cassia
Celery
Cinnamon

Clary Sage
Cloves
Cucumber
Damiana
Dandelion
Dittany
Frankincense
Ginger
Gotu Kola

Hibiscus
Honeysuckle
Hyssop
Lavender
Lemon Balm
Lemon Grass
Lilac
Mandrake
Marigold

(Psychic Development and Growth cont.)

Marjoram	Rosemary	Spearmint
Menthol	Rue	Star Anise
Mugwort	Safflower	Sunflower
Nutmeg	Sage	Thyme
Oregano	Sandalwood	Wisteria
Parsley	Solomon's Seal	Wormwood
Peppermint	Southernwood	Yerba Santa

Psychic Protection

Prevents harm from evil or negative forces; safeguards against outside influences.

Agrimony	Galangal	Rose
Angelica	Ginger	Geranium
Anise	Hemlock	Rue
Asafoetida	Hyssop	Sage
Basil	Lemon	St. Johnswort
Bay	Verbena	Salep
Benzoin	Lilac	Solomon's Seal
Broom	Lovage	Spikenard
Cinquefoil	Marjoram	Spruce
Clover	Melilot	Star Anise
Cloves	Mistletoe	Storax
Cranesbill	Mugwort	Valerian
Dill	Myrrh	Vetiver
Dragon's	Nettle	Wood Betony
Blood	Oregano	Woodruff
Elder	Patchouli	Wood Sorrel
Fennel	Pine	Wormwood
Frankincense	Red Clover	Yarrow

Release and Endings

Sets free from restraint, restrictions, and unwanted events or situations; removes pain, trouble, worry, and grief; successful completion of a goal; release from unwanted involvements.

Asafoetida	Menthol	Slippery Elm
Bay	Myrrh	Spearmint
Camphor	Pennyroyal	Water Lily
Comfrey	Peppermint	Willow
Lemon Balm	Quassia	Woodruff
Melilot	Rosemary	Yarrow

Renewal

Causes healing and regeneration; health and vitality; return or increase of strength; restore, rebuild, or revive ideas, plans, things, etc.

Allspice	Ground Ivy	Peppermint
Aloe	Hemlock	Pomegranate
Angelica	Henna	Primrose
Eucalyptus	Holly	Spearmint
Ginseng	Marigold	Water Lily
Gotu Kola	Mistletoe	Woodruff

Retention

Prevents loss; keeps secure; to retain what is rightfully yours.

Agrimony	Coriander	Dogwood
Caraway	Crabgrass	Ground Ivy
Clary Sage	Dill	Honeysuckle

(Retention cont.)

Horehound	Life	Rose
Juniper	Everlasting	Sage
Lavender	Oak	Sarsaparilla
	Pomegranate	Tarragon

Sensuality

Increases passion, sex appeal, and pleasure; causes attraction, lust, and physical love.

Ambergris	Ginger	Rose
Basil	Jasmine	Geranium
Bergamot	Mandrake	Savory
Caraway	Musk	Saw Palmetto
Cascarilla	Musk Root	Tarragon
Civit	Mustard	Tumeric
Cranesbill	Patchouli	Yohimbe
Damiana	Pepperweed	

Stop Gossip

Protects reputation; stops idle speculation; guards against slander; negates negative statements and remarks.

Chickweed	Garlic	Psyllium
Clover	Onion	Red Clover
Cloves	Orris	Rose
Cranesbill	Plantain	Geranium
Deer's	Primrose	Slippery Elm
Tongue		

Strength

Increases legal, moral, or intellectual power; gives strength, stamina, and vitality; protects strength; enhances physical well-being.

Aloe	Ginseng	Oak
Balm of	Hemlock	Pine
Gilead	Honeysuckle	Red Clover
Basil	Juniper	Rosemary
Bergamot	Lemon	St. Johnswort
Camomile	Lemon Grass	Spruce
Cedar	Melilot	Storax
Clover	Mugwort	Tarragon
Dragon's	Musk	Turmeric
Blood	Musk Root	Uva Ursi
Fennel	Mustard	Yerba Santa
Garlic		

Success

Favorable outcome to project, event, or situation; luck; prosperity; attainment; reach a goal, causes gain, wealth, victory, and achievement.

Angelica	Marigold	Sandalwood
Basil	Mistletoe	Scammony
Bergamot	Musk	Solomon's
Cedar	Musk Root	Seal
Frankincense	Mustard	Storax
Garlic	Myrrh	Sunflower
Grains of	Oak	Sweet Gum
Paradise	Onion	Vervain
Jalap	St. Johnswort	Vetiver
Lemon	Salep	Woodruff
Verbena		

Transformation

Change nature, conditions, functions, personality and character;
to convert, modify, or shift one's life.

Bay	Plantain	Spearmint
Elder	Psyllium	Vervain
Frankincense	Rose	Violet
Holly	Rosemary	Woodruff
Myrrh	Southernwood	Wormwood
Peppermint		

Virility

Increase of masculine strength, vigor, stamina.

Ambergris	Holly	Mustard
Balm of	Lavender	Oak
Gilead	Mandrake	Savory
Cascarilla	Mistletoe	Tarragon
Civit	Musk	Vetiver
Dragon's Blood	Musk Root	

Weddings

Ensures contentment and happiness; encourages proposals;
fulfillment, satisfaction, and success of the couple.

Broom	Linden	Oregano
Ground Ivy	Marjoram	Rose
Honeysuckle	Meadowsweet	Rosemary
Jasmine	Myrtle	Sage
Lady's Mantle	Orange	Yarrow

APPENDIX 7

WEIGHTS & MEASURES

Solid

60 Grains	= 1 Teaspoon (t)
3 Teaspoons	= 1 Tablespoon (T)
2 Tablespoons	= 1 Ounce (Oz)
4 Ounces	= 1 Gill
2 Gills	= 1 Cup (C)
2 Cups	= 1 Pint

Liquid

60 Drops	= 1 Teaspoon (t)
3 Teaspoons	= 1 Tablespoon (T)
2 Tablespoons	= 1 Fluid Ounce
4 Fluid Oz.	= 1 Gill
2 Gills	= 1 Cup (C)
2 Cups	= 1 Pint

Apothecaries' Measure

60 Minims (Drops)	= 1 Fluid Dram
8 Fluid Drams	= 1 Fluid Ounce
8 Fluid Ounces	= 1 Cup
16 Fluid Ounces	= 1 Pint

Fractions of a Cup

1/4 Cup = 4 Tablespoons
1/3 Cup = 5 Tablespoons + 1 Teaspoon
1/2 Cup = 8 Tablespoons
2/3 Cup = 10 Tablespoons + 2 Teaspoons
3/4 Cup = 12 Tablespoons
1 Cup = 16 Tablespoons

Saltpeter Formulas

QB = 1/2 Cup Water + 1/4 teaspoon Saltpeter (SP)
FW = 2 Tablespoons + 2 teaspoons Water + 1/4 teaspoon SP
LF = 1 Tablespoon + 1 teaspoon Water + 1/4 teaspoon SP

Approximate Weight of Herbs per Cup

Bark . . . . .4 ounces
Berries . . . . .4 ounces
Flowers . . . . .2 ounces
Leaves . . . . .2 ounces
Powdered Herbs . . . . .4 ounces
Roots . . . . .4 ounces
Seeds . . . . .4 ounces
Whole Herbs . . . . .2 ounces

Olde Grimoire Measurements (Approximate)

Double Handful = $1\frac{1}{2}$ Cups
Handful   = $\frac{2}{3}$ Cup
Fistful   = $\frac{1}{3}$ Cup
Palm   = $\frac{1}{4}$ Cup
Three Fingers = $3\frac{1}{2}$ Teaspoons
Two Fingers = 1 Teaspoon
Pinch   = $\frac{1}{8}$ Teaspoon

BIBLIOGRAPHY

Barret, Francis. *The Magus*. Secaucus, NJ: Citadel, 1977.

Birren, Faber. *Color Psychology and Color Therapy*. New Hyde Park, NY: University Books, 1961.

Buckland, Raymond. *Practical Candleburning Rituals*. St. Paul, MN: Llewellyn, 1978.

Conway, David. *Magic: An Occult Primer*. New York: E. P. Dutton, 1972.

_____. *The Magic of Herbs*. New York: E. P. Dutton, 1973.

Crow, W. B. *The Occult Properties of Herbs and Plants*. York Beach, ME: Samuel Weiser, 1980; Wellingborough, England: Aquarian Press, 1980.

Crowley, Aleister. *Magick: In Theory and Practice*. New York: Dover, 1976; York Beach, ME: Samuel Weiser, 1974; London: Arcana, 1973.

Culpepper, Nicholas. *Culpeper's Complete Herbal*. London: Foulsham, 1981.

Cunningham, Scott. *Magical Herbalism*. St. Paul, MN: Llewellyn, 1981.

Frazer, James, G. *The Golden Bough*. New York: Macmillan, 1951.

Graves, Robert. *The White Goddess*. New York: Farrar, Straus, & Giroux, 1976.

Grieve, M. *A Modern Herbal*. New York: Dover, 1971.

Grimm, William Carey. *Home Guide to Trees, Shrubs, and Wildflowers*. New York: Bonanza Books, 1970.

Huson, Paul. *Mastering Herbalism*. New York: Stein & Day, 1975.

_____. *Mastering Witchcraft*. New York: Berkley, 1977.

Lust, John. *The Herb Book*. New York: Bantam, 1974.

Martin, Alexander C. *Weeds*. New York: Golden Press, 1972.

Mathers, S. L. *The Key of Solomon the King*. York Beach, ME: Samuel Weiser, 1976; London: Arkana, 1976.

Millspaugh, Charles F. *American Medicinal Plants*. New York: Dover, 1974.

Simmons, Adelma Grenier. *A Witch's Brew*. Tolland, CT: Clinton Press, 1981.

Thompson, C. J. S. *The Mystery and Lore of Perfume*. Detroit, MI: Singing Tree Press, 1969.

Tisserand, Robert B. *The Art of Aromatherapy*. Rochester, VT: Inner Traditions, 1979; Saffron Walden, UK: C. W. Daniel, 1979.

Tucker, Ann. *Potpourri, Incense, and Other Fragrant Concoctions*. New York: Workman, 1972.

Vinci, Leo. *Incense: Its Ritual Significance, Use, and Preparation*. York Beach, ME: Samuel Weiser, 1980; Wellingborough, England: Aquarian Press, 1980.

Waite, Arthur, E. *The Book of Ceremonial Magic*. Secaucus, NJ: Citadel, 1973.

_____. *Complete Manual of Occult Divination*. New Hyde Park, NY: University Books, 1972.

Winter, Ruth. *A Consumer's Dictionary of Cosmetic Ingredients*. New York: Crown, 1976.

Wright, Elbee. *Book of Legendary Spells*. Minneapolis, MN: Marlar, 1974.